BRUTAL LESSONS IN RESILIENCE EVERY
LEADER CAN LEARN FROM ENTREPRENEURS

PERCHED IN THE STORM

DR. WILLIAM T. LEWIS

SPARK Publications
Charlotte, North Carolina

Perched in the Storm
Brutal Lessons in Resilience Every Leader
Can Learn from Entrepreneurs
Dr. William T. Lewis

Scripture quotations are taken from the New King James Version®.
Copyright © 1982 by Thomas Nelson. All rights reserved.

Designed, produced, and published by
SPARK Publications
SPARKpublications.com
Charlotte, North Carolina

Printed in the United States of America

Paperback, January 2026, ISBN: 978-1-968760-99-1
Library of Congress Control Number: 2025927161

Dedication

Tash—welp, this is my second "coloring" book.
Thank you for perching beside me in the storm!

Acknowledgments

I want to say a huge thank you to the ten incredible folks (**Allan, Magalie, Starlight, Ta'Nisha, Keith, Rod, Fabi, John, Ciandress, and Tasha**) who generously shared their time and voices for this project.

Listening to and reading your stories has taught me so much. Your experiences made me feel less alone in my own entrepreneurial journey. I hope our readers learn from you and feel just as inspired by you as I am.

SECTION ONE

SECTION TWO

PART 5: WEATHER REPORTS FROM THE STORM CHASERS

SECTION THREE

PART 6: LIGHTHOUSE IN THE STORM

EPILOGUE: PERCHED WITH PURPOSE

INTRODUCTION

PERCHED IN THE STORM

For eighteen months, the working title of this book was *This Shit Ain't Easy: Leadership Lessons From the Eyes of an Entrepreneur.* I was emotionally invested in that title. It felt raw, provocative, and powerful. I believed it would resonate deeply with the people I wrote this book for—leaders who know firsthand how tough the climb can be. The sentiment was clear: Entrepreneurship isn't easy, leadership isn't easy, and navigating both is an uphill battle.

But while the title captured the truth, it also created barriers. My publisher, Fabi Preslar, said it best: "Will, with that kind of profanity in your main title, you won't get invited to churches, schools, or mainstream business conferences. Libraries won't carry the book, and Facebook, Google, and LinkedIn may not even let you promote it." Darn, Fabi, you know how to burst a bubble!

At first, I resisted. That title felt like *me*. It felt like my story. But then I did what resilient leaders have to do: I took a step back, asked myself what this book is really about, and listened to wise counsel. After some reflection (and a few grumbles to my wife), I realized the message was more important than my attachment to any one phrase. I needed a title that captured the rawness of the entrepreneurial experience without getting in the way of sharing it.

So, I started pivoting—because pivoting is part of resilience too. I tried *Leading in the Eye*, which leaned into the storm metaphor I wanted to make, but it felt more like a mystery novel than a book on resilience and leadership. Then came the "mic drop" moment. Fabi suggested *Perched in the Storm: Brutal Lessons In Resilience Every Leader Can Learn From Entrepreneurs.*

Boom! That was it. It spoke to my soul. It aligned with a rebrand into resilient leadership. It was evocative, true to my experience, and grounded in a powerful image—one that I've come back to again and again.

Imagine a storm—violent winds, dark skies, pounding rain—and picture a bird perched on a branch, unbothered. That bird doesn't ignore the storm, but it doesn't panic either. Its feathers are ruffled, its body drenched, but it holds steady—alert, grounded, ready to fly when the time is right. That's resilience.

This image powerfully illustrates the human experience of endurance during the chaos of the storm. But what's not as obvious is the hidden story behind the branch and the tree itself. That strength didn't happen by chance.

Not long ago, I was sharing the title of this book with a colleague, and he responded with something unexpected. "Have you heard about Biosphere 2?" he asked. I hadn't. I almost nodded because it sounded like something from a science lesson and I should've paid more attention in high school—but, in the end, I was truthful and said no. He explained it to me, and afterward, I dug into it and discovered an interesting connection between wind, trees, and resilience.

For those of you who are like me and may not be aware of Biosphere 2, it was a sealed, self-sustaining ecosystem in Arizona designed to replicate Earth's environment (Biosphere 1) and explore how life might be supported in space or on other planets. Inside this massive glass dome, scientists created rainforests, deserts, oceans—and planted trees. And those trees grew fast. With abundant sunlight and water and no pests, they shot up tall and straight. But then something strange happened.

Many of the trees collapsed under their own weight before reaching maturity. The reason? No wind. Without the pressure and resistance of wind, the trees failed to develop what scientists call **"stress wood"**—a type of structural tissue produced in response to mechanical stress (Telewski, 1995). In nature, wind bends a tree again and again, prompting it to reinforce its internal structure and anchor itself more deeply in the soil. The very force that seems like a threat is what gives the tree its strength (Niklas, 1992).

That's the paradox of resilience—a paradox that is hard to remember when you're perched in the storm.

Trees exposed to wind don't just survive—they *adapt*. Their roots dig deeper, gripping harder. Their trunks widen at the base, developing a kind of muscular memory that allows them to bend without breaking. Their branches grow stronger joints, reinforced with **stress wood**, capable of withstanding both the gusts of wind and the weight of whatever life places upon them—even a cardinal in the rain (Niklas, 1992; Telewski, 1995).

Like those trees, we humans grow strong not in the absence of stress but because of it. It's in the winds of adversity—grief, loss, failure, uncertainty—that we dig our roots deeper. We discover the strength of our foundation: our values, our purpose, our community. The storms don't just test us—they shape us. They show us who we are.

So, when you see that bird perched on the branch, remember: It's not just the bird that's resilient. The branch is too. And the branch holds because the tree has weathered storms before—because it has stress wood in its limbs, deep roots in the earth, and strength born from struggle.

There is perhaps a divine parallel between nature and the human experience. We, too, are perched in the storm. We are

held up by the deep-rooted strength of our communities, our families, our mentors, our lived experiences.

Friends, this book isn't a technical manual on entrepreneurship or leadership theory. It's not a textbook or a polished how-to guide. There are plenty of those at your local bookstore. This book is about the real stuff—the kind forged in the windstorms of life:

- Failing 100 times and discovering the breakthrough happens on the 101st
- Turning rejection into redirection
- Staying grounded when your vision feels like it's slipping away
- Leading with heart, grit, and authenticity when the spreadsheet says "walk away"

The Storms I've Faced

I didn't just write this book as a business coach or leadership consultant. I wrote it as someone who's lived through the mess. I was fired from my nine-to-five, forced to leap into entrepreneurship without a soft landing. I had always dreamed of working for myself, but the reality was nothing like the fantasy.

Here's just a sample of the storms I've weathered:

- Opening a coffee shop in what seemed like a prime location—only to find out foot traffic was nonexistent.
- Watching loyal customers quietly vanish without explanation. They call this "ghosting."
- Investing $20,000 into developing new technology, only to watch it flop—while my wife gave me the side-eye over dinner.
- Having a $20,000 month followed by three $2,000 months and realizing I may need to get a "real job" … again. Eventually, I did!

And yet, still perched. Still persevering. Still thriving.

What Is Resilience?

Resilience "is the process and outcome of successfully adapting to difficult or challenging life experiences, especially through mental, emotional, and behavioral flexibility and adjustment to external and internal demands. A number of factors contribute to how well people adapt to adversities, including the ways in which individuals view and engage with the world, the availability and quality of social resources, and specific coping strategies" (American Psychological Association Dictionary of Psychology, https://dictionary.apa.org/resilience).

What Makes Entrepreneurs So Resilient?

Entrepreneurs are problem solvers, risk takers, and resource creators. They're constantly navigating ambiguity, scarcity, and setbacks. According to the U.S. Small Business Administration, small businesses make up 99.9 percent of all U.S. firms, employ nearly half the workforce, and contribute around 44 percent of U.S. GDP. These are the leaders keeping our economy moving—and often doing it without a safety net.

So, what can every leader learn from entrepreneurs? Plenty.

Entrepreneurs don't wait for perfect conditions. They move forward with conviction, flexibility, and urgency. That mindset—what I call "entrepreneurial resilience"—isn't just useful when you're starting a business. It's essential when you're leading in a world like ours, where the next storm is always forming on the horizon.

What COVID-19 Taught Us About Resilience Leadership

Between 2020 and 2025, we lived through one of the greatest leadership stress tests of our time. The COVID-19 pandemic wasn't just a health crisis—it was a leadership crucible. More than 6.9 million lives were lost globally. Economies were shut down. Nonprofits collapsed. Supply chains broke. Burnout surged. Our family coffee shop, Cam's, was forced to close its doors; we had to send our workers home, and our hearts were crushed!

But amid the chaos, a new model of leadership emerged. It wasn't about being the loudest voice in the room or having the right answer every time. It was about doing the following:

- Leading with empathy
- Listening more than speaking
- Acting decisively despite having incomplete information
- Adapting, learning, and iterating on the fly
- Putting well-being at the center of team performance

Studies, surveys, and firsthand experiences confirm it: The leaders who thrived during COVID didn't do so because they were the smartest in the room. They did so because they were resilient.

Through the lens of COVID and entrepreneurship, I've distilled seven powerful behaviors of resilient leaders. I will unpack these in detail in **Part 6: Lighthouse in the Storm**. For now, I will provide a high-level highlight of each behavior.

1. Mindset Mastery

You can't lead others well if you can't lead your own mind. Resilient leaders know that mindset is not a motivational poster—it's a discipline. It's choosing progress over perfection, abundance over scarcity, and courage over comfort. Mastering your mindset is how you stay perched when everything around you says to panic.

2. Adaptability

Things rarely go as planned. Storms will come. Customers will disappear. Teams will shift. Budgets will get cut. The question is not, "Will change happen?" It's, "Will you bend, or will you break?" Resilient leaders pivot without losing their purpose. As we say in the Marine Corps, resilient leaders need to "adapt, improvise, and overcome … Oorah!"

3. Emotional Intelligence

IQ might get you the job, but Emotional Intelligence helps you keep your people. In times of uncertainty, empathy, self-awareness, and emotional regulation are leadership superpowers. The entrepreneurs I interview in this book don't just understand the strategy—they understand the temperature in the room and the story behind the struggle.

4. Strategic Career Growth

Too many leaders wait for permission to grow. Resilient leaders take ownership of their development. They understand their value, set boundaries, seek mentorship, and position themselves to thrive. Career resilience isn't just about climbing the ladder—it's about building a life and legacy you're proud of.

5. Continuous Growth and Innovation

If you're not learning, you're losing. The most resilient entrepreneurs I know never stop iterating. They test, refine, evolve. They make space for creativity and aren't afraid to break what isn't working—even if they built it themselves. Innovation isn't reserved for tech companies; it's a survival skill for every leader.

6. Service-Oriented Leadership
Real leadership is about others. Full stop. It's about empowering, uplifting, and equipping your people to do meaningful work. Entrepreneurs get this—they know their success is tied to how well they serve. Resilient leaders lead with a posture of service, not ego.

7. Work–Life Integration
The hustle culture taught us to burn out in silence. Resilient leadership rejects that. You cannot pour from an empty cup. Integration doesn't mean balancing every day—it means knowing your capacity, setting boundaries, and designing a life where your values aren't just slogans, they're practiced.

Why This Book and Why Now
The next chapter of leadership won't be written with the tools of the past.

We are currently facing continued disruption—driven by forces that are reshaping every sector, every system, and every skill set we once thought was future-proof. One of the most significant of these forces is the rapid acceleration of artificial intelligence (AI), a defining feature of what the World Economic Forum has identified as the Fourth Industrial Revolution (Schwab, 2016).

A brief recap of the four industrial revolutions for those sitting in the back row, like me:

1. **First Industrial Revolution** – *Mechanical production powered by water and steam.*

2. **Second** – *Mass production enabled by electricity.*

3. **Third** – *The digital revolution, driven by computers and automation.*

4. **Fourth (Now)** – *Cyber-physical systems that merge the physical, digital, and biological spheres—driven by breakthroughs in AI, robotics, biotechnology, and quantum computing.*

In this fourth revolution, **AI isn't just evolving—it's transforming how we live, work, and lead.**

Did you know you can now develop your own "AI Board of Directors"? This blew me away!

My wife has built herself a digital advisory council—custom-trained AI models that provide perspective on some of her biggest leadership questions. These AI advisors can help you think through strategy, manage complex decisions, rehearse difficult conversations, or simply challenge your blind spots.

Leadership in this new era won't be about resisting change—it will be about learning to partner with it. Those who thrive will be the ones who are bold enough to start, curious enough to explore, and humble enough to adapt.

This book is for you—the emerging leader, the seasoned executive, the burned-out nonprofit director, the department head, the solopreneur. This book is a "right now book." This book is to help you get ready and stay ready to lead through the next storm. This book is your lighthouse. Because, friends, this shit ain't easy. But you? You are built for this.

You're perched in the storm.

How to Navigate This Book

This book is structured around three leadership journeys, each offering a unique lens into the realities of building resilience in the face of adversity.

- **Parts 1–4** take you through *my personal storms*—the raw, unfiltered lessons I've learned as a leader and entrepreneur navigating uncertainty and change.
- **Part 5** amplifies the voices of *fellow entrepreneurs* who've weathered their own storms, offering hard-earned wisdom and diverse perspectives on what it means to lead with resilience.
- **Part 6** delivers a *practical framework* designed to help you apply the principles of resilient leadership to your own life and work—because reflection without action isn't enough.

Each journey builds upon the last: from personal struggle, to shared experience, to strategic application. Whether you're leading a business or a team or simply trying to navigate a difficult season, this book meets you where you are.

- If you're looking for motivation and personal connection, begin with **Parts 1–4**.
- If you want insight from other resilient leaders, go straight to **Part 5**.
- And if you're ready for actionable tools to lead through chaos, **Part 6** is your roadmap.

You can read it straight through or start where you feel most drawn.

No matter where you begin, you'll end with the same truth: **Storms are inevitable, but resilient leaders don't just survive them—they rise because of them.**

PART 1: Eye of the Idea

"Every storm starts with a shift in the wind. So does every dream."

In this section, I dive into how every idea begins in our mind. We have to imagine it before we can bring it to life. As you read this, think about your own dreams and the sparks of inspiration that have crossed your mind. How do you take those initial ideas and turn them into something real? This part will help you explore how to tap into your own vision and bring your thoughts to life, even when the winds of doubt try to blow them away.

PART 2: Direct Hit

"The thunder doesn't ask if you're ready."

In this section, I explore the defining entrepreneurial moments that shaped me. You'll recognize these moments, as they are part of your journey too. Whether it's a sudden challenge or a major turning point, we all face those "direct hit" experiences. How do you handle the moments when everything changes in an instant? This section will guide you through understanding how those hits—unexpected and brutal—can shape you into a stronger leader.

PART 3: A Perfect Storm

"When several adversities collide, they create a perfect storm—not to destroy you but to reveal the strength you didn't know you had."

This section explores the moments when multiple challenges collide—personally, professionally, emotionally—creating what feels like an unstoppable wave of adversity. I open up about the times when everything seemed to unravel at once, when I felt overwhelmed, disoriented, and uncertain about what would come next. These aren't just tough moments—they're defining ones. When the pressure builds from all directions, we're forced to dig deeper than we thought possible. This part reveals how, even in your most chaotic seasons, resilience can take root and begin to transform your leadership and your life.

PART 4: Rebuilding in the Rain

"You can't stop the storm, but you can rebuild in the rain."

This section highlights my resilience, determination, and sheer willpower to keep going. But this isn't just my story—it's yours too. Every leader faces setbacks, but it's how you rebuild during those times that truly matters. This section will show you how to find the strength and determination to keep pushing forward, even when the storm hasn't passed. No matter how tough things may seem, you will learn how to rebuild with purpose and clarity.

PART 5: Weather Reports from the Storm Chasers

"Some people chase the sun. Entrepreneurs chase storms—and learn to build in them."

This section features conversations with entrepreneurs and people from the entrepreneurial support ecosystem. Their insights will resonate with you, showing that the challenges and highs of the entrepreneurial journey are universal. We all face storms, but we also learn how to navigate them. As you read their stories, ask yourself, how can you apply these lessons to your own leadership journey, especially when you're navigating through your own storm?

PART 6: Lighthouse in the Storm

"True leaders don't just survive the storm; they shine through it—so others know where to go."

In this section, I introduce the Resilient Leader Framework—a practical guide to recognizing and embodying the key behaviors of resilient leadership. This framework is built on the rich, real-life stories shared throughout this book and supported by research on what makes leaders thrive in adversity. It's designed to help you lead with clarity, strength, and purpose—even when the storm is at its worst.

EPILOGUE: Perched with Purpose

"You weren't meant to outrun the storm. You were built to stand in the middle of it."

This section is about hope and triumph—about surviving adversity and emerging even stronger. Ultimately, this book is a celebration of resilience, the will to survive, and the determination to never give up. It's about you and your own path forward. How will you stand firm when the storm rages around you? The storms you face are not the end but the beginning of something new. This final section is your invitation to embrace your resilience and rise above, no matter what challenges come your way.

We grow
strong, not in
the absence of
stress but in
the presence
of it.

SECTION ONE

PART 1

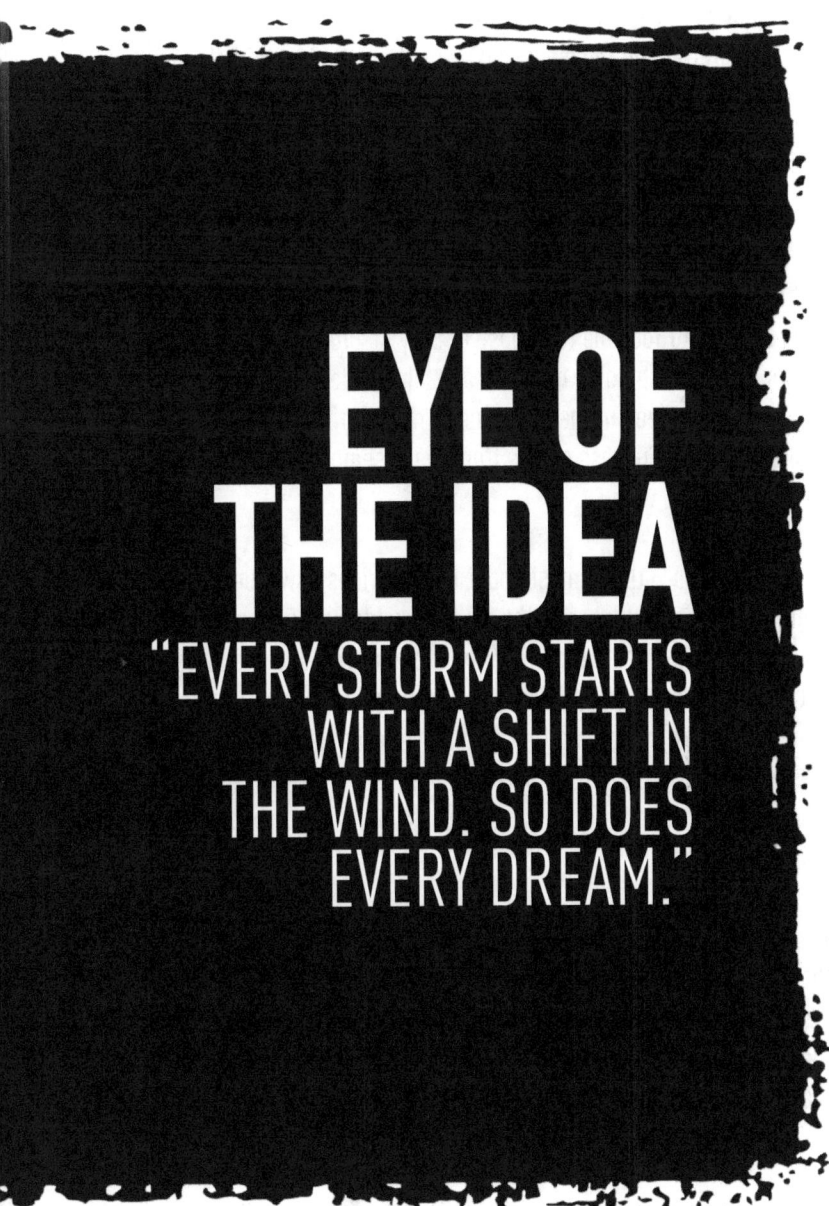

EYE OF THE IDEA

"EVERY STORM STARTS WITH A SHIFT IN THE WIND. SO DOES EVERY DREAM."

In this section, I explore how every dream starts with a single thought. Before anything becomes real, it must first be imagined. As you read, pause and reflect on the ideas and inspirations that have flickered through your mind. What would it take to bring them to life? This part will guide you in harnessing your vision and shaping it into something tangible—even when doubt tries to cloud your clarity.

When my spirits have been beat down by the strong winds of adversity and I need a solid dose of motivation to help me get up off the mat, I head straight to YouTube for a dose of Billy Alsbrooks's "Blessed and Unstoppable" (Alsbrooks, n.d.). It's a mashup video of spoken word over music that hits deep in the soul. One of my favorite lines from Billy's spoken word is "Success comes from the assembly line of my mind." I love this verse!

What resonates with me most about Billy's lyric is how true it is: Everything we see and use in the physical world was first created in the mind before it ever came to life in the material world. The successful entrepreneur is always imagining—imagining a new way to do an old thing, imagining something that doesn't yet exist, imagining how to make an idea bigger, better, more efficient, and more convenient. Entrepreneurs are masterful at seeing possibilities where others see only obstacles.

Which brings me back to the storm. Every storm starts with a shift in the wind. And every dream starts with a shift in the imagination. The first thing leaders can learn from entrepreneurs is to nurture a mindset that sees things differently, that embraces the calm of imagination—the kind of calm where ideas and solutions are born.

"You Are Not Sitting at a Table?!"

It was my first year in college when my philosophy professor asked, "Is this a table?" I looked around at my peers in this introduction to philosophy course, and then I muttered to myself, "What in the h.a.i.l. have I gotten myself into?" (Side note: That was not the first nor last time I've asked myself that question. In fact, I recently said yes to taking on a new client, and this very question came to me like a raging river! I digress. Back to philosophy.)

"Yes, we are sitting around a table," I mumbled (somewhat annoyed) in a low voice for only my ears to hear. You know, like how you used to speak when you didn't want your parents to hear you! My professor was introducing us to Plato's theory of forms, which, put simply, says that what we see in the material world—the real world—is just a shadow of a more perfect, ideal version of things that exist in our minds. In other words, the perfect "table" exists as an idea in our imagination before it ever gets made into the physical table we're sitting around. So, while we're all gathered around what we call a "table," Plato would argue that we're not really sitting at a true table. What we're looking at is just a flawed copy of the perfect "table-ness" that exists only in our minds (Plato, trans. 1991).

It took me a minute to wrap my head around it—well, actually, fifty years—but the biggest lesson I took away from my freshman philosophy class wasn't just about abstract ideas and ideal forms. It was this: Solutions are found first in our imagination. Before anything becomes real—before it's tangible, before it's materialized—it starts as an idea. In other words, if you want to innovate, the first step is to imagine the perfect solution, even if it's not something you can touch or see yet. Once you have that vision, only then can you begin to build it.

I heard Bishop T. D. Jakes express this point from a spiritual perspective this way (note: I am paraphrasing): God made the trees. He did not make the tables. He gave humans the imagination and the raw materials (the trees). By using their imagination, humans made tables from the raw materials.

Noodle on that one for a minute.

When most entrepreneurs start their business, they have a lot of imagination and few raw materials: a single baking recipe from Big Mamma, but no ingredients, a pair of shears and clippers but no building, coding skills but no hardware from which to create code, and coffee beans but no espresso machine. They take their raw materials and imagine what they could be. And then born into the world are Sifted Sugar, Gifted Hands, Once Logic, and Cam's Coffee Co. (You will see these companies in **Part 5: Weather Reports from the Storm Chasers**).

You Are the One Who Bends!

To turn your imagination into an assembly line of ideas, you must upend some of your rigid mindsets. Do you remember in *The Matrix* when Neo visits the Oracle for the first time? He is instructed to wait in the living room, which is filled with others who are being evaluated to see if they are the "One." Neo approaches a kid sitting on the floor holding a spoon. He observes the spoon bending. Neo is amazed by what he sees, but the boy tells Neo that it is not the spoon that is bending—because there is no spoon (this brought back memories of my philosophy class). Rather, it is Neo who is bending. The boy is trying to help Neo realize that he can manipulate the rules in the Matrix with his mind. The more he releases rigid thinking about what he can do, the more powerful he becomes (Wachowski & Wachowski, 1999).

Similarly, I came to realize that once I released a fixed mindset and grasped hold of an entrepreneurial mindset, I could bend the rules that govern the status quo (routine, predictability, and stability) and unlock the potential hidden in my imagination that would transform me and the world around me. But this is easier said than done.

Throughout both my nine-to-five and entrepreneurial careers, I've always looked for ways to fill gaps and provide solutions. For example, while working on my doctorate, I was employed at two universities, and I had the opportunity to witness firsthand the struggles first-year students had with adjusting to university life. Not by coincidence, my dissertation focused on the factors that influenced the success of African American students at predominantly White institutions, primarily in their first semester. Specifically, I studied students who—like me during my undergraduate years—were the first in their immediate families to attend college and came from low socioeconomic backgrounds.

The next logical and traditional step after completing a doctorate is to revise the dissertation for publication—either as a book or in a peer-reviewed journal. Sometimes I am not logical or traditional, hence the first title I had for this book. Instead of going the academic publishing route, I turned my dissertation into an educational board game (this was before online gaming) designed for high school seniors and first-year college students.

The game, First Semester, foreshadowed the expectations and experiences of a student's first semester in college. I didn't dominate the market, but I sold a few hundred copies from the thousand-unit minimum order I had to place with a U.S.-based game manufacturer. More importantly, I experienced that ping (hold on to this, I will explain in a later chapter)—the thrill of seeing something I imagined come to life in the real world.

So, I realized that I couldn't just work within the limits of what exists—I had to imagine what could be and bring it to life. Every breakthrough, innovation, or disruptive idea starts in the mind before it manifests in the world. Whether it's reimagining an old process, spotting an overlooked gap, or challenging the status quo, success stems from the willingness to think differently and embrace an entrepreneurial mindset.

But unlocking this level of creativity and innovation requires more than just great ideas—it demands a willingness to bend. Just as Neo in *The Matrix* had to release rigid thinking to unlock his power, I had to let go of fixed mindsets and embrace a world where I can shape new possibilities. This is the key to turning raw materials— whether they be skills, knowledge, or passion—into something transformational.

Friends, the journey of turning imagination into reality is not always smooth, and the path is rarely predictable. But for those who dare to imagine, question, and create, the rewards are immense. Just as every storm starts with a shift in the wind, every great idea begins with a shift in the imagination. Whether it's building a business, reshaping an industry, or simply finding a new way to solve a problem, it all begins in the calm of the mind, before the storm of execution hits. For you, this means leaning into the power of imagination—not just for yourself but also for your team. When you cultivate a space where your team feels empowered to imagine, explore, and challenge the status quo, you create a storm of creativity that will inevitably lead to innovation.

Every breakthrough, innovation, or disruptive idea starts in the mind before it manifests in the world.

PART 2:

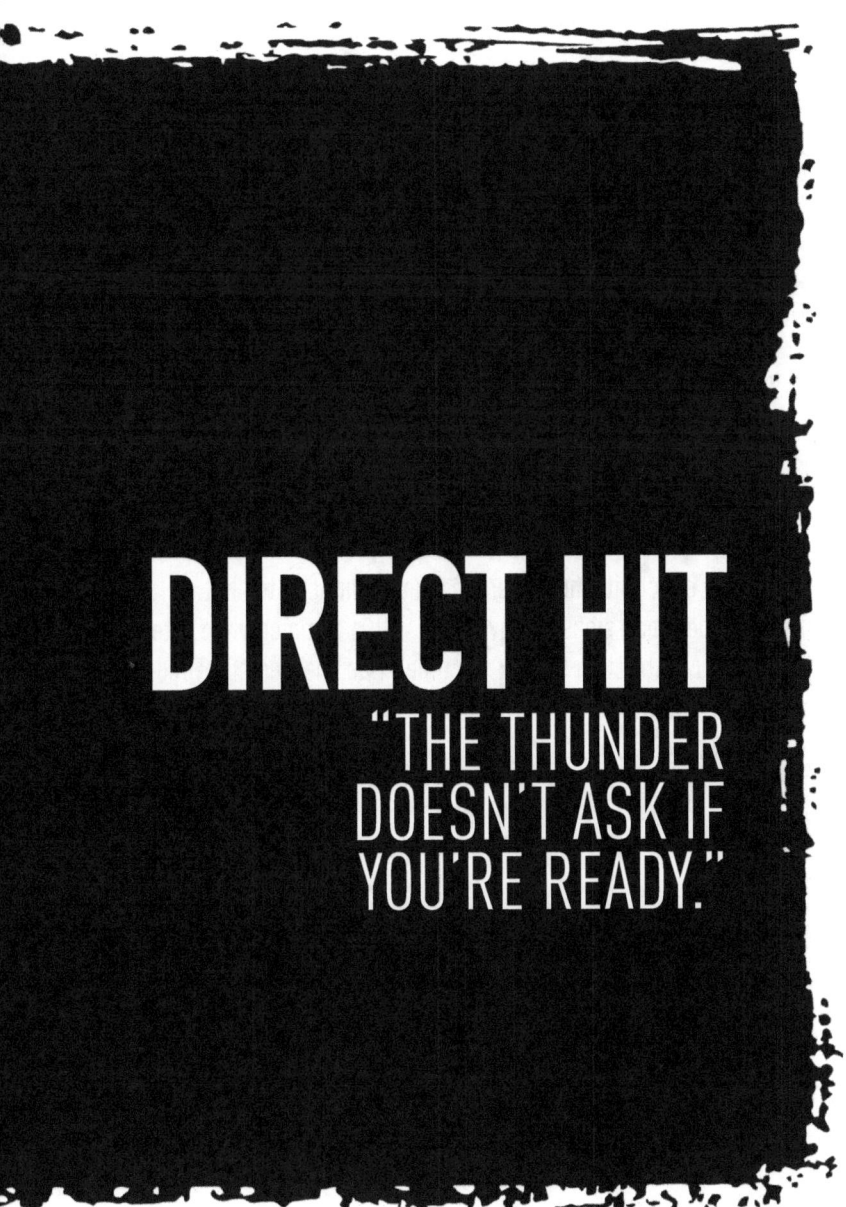

DIRECT HIT

"THE THUNDER DOESN'T ASK IF YOU'RE READY."

This section dives into the lightning-strike moments that cracked open the entrepreneur in me. I wasn't born thinking like a boss or raised in a house full of business moguls. I became an entrepreneur the hard way—through the storm.

It took a few direct hits, both literal and metaphorical, to shift my path—like the time I smashed my thumb with a hammer while helping my dad on a construction site. Or the time I was unexpectedly fired from my six-figure dream job. Thunder doesn't knock. It just crashes in—and you respond, or you crumble.

Hit the Nail, Not Your Thumb

It was about zero dark thirty (that's military talk for real early and still dark), and my dad and I were packing our lunches—bologna sandwiches, Doritos, Oreos, a Pepsi, and a big dill pickle (gotta get your veggies). We threw the cooler and his tools into his olive green '76 Ford F-150. At ten years old, I could've listed a hundred things I'd rather be doing on my summer break than heading to a job site.

But going to work with my dad, a master carpenter, was special. I didn't know much about hammers and nails, but I knew I loved being in his presence. I visited him in the summers and on weekends, and when I turned sixteen, I moved in with him full time.

Now, you'd think with all that time on job sites, and living with him, that some of his carpentry skills would've rubbed off. Nope. Nada. Not even a little.

One day, he handed me a hammer and told me to nail two pieces of plywood together, probably just to keep me busy. Once he heard the high-pitched yelp that escaped my mouth, I'm sure he abandoned whatever project he was focused on.

I had hit my thumb—squarely, painfully, comically. OUCH. You ever done that? Yeah … you feel it in your soul.

That was pretty much the end of my "career" as a construction helper. After that, I still visited job sites, but I kept my distance from anything with a blade or a nail. Right then and there, I made a pact with myself: I was not going to work with my hands. I would pay someone to fix my faucet, build my bookshelf, or change my oil.

But here's the thing—I knew if I was going to pay folks to do the things I couldn't (or wouldn't) do, then I had better find a way to get paid in full.

I Want to Be Paid in Full

I came of age in the '80s—a time of latchkey kids, breakdancing, Cyndi Lauper's neon hair, MC Hammer pants, and boom boxes blasting hip-hop. Money was tight. My mom, sister, and I didn't have designer anything. When Polo was hot at school, my mom bought me a shirt with a man sitting on a horse. It was … not the same. That shirt saw daylight once.

By 1987, I was in high school, rocking baggy pants and a polka dot shirt, headed to my business class, Walkman in tow. My theme music? *Paid in Full* by Eric B. and Rakim.

The entire rap is solid, with banging beats and not a curse word from start to finish. However, there are a few lyrics that resonate with me the most. The line "Thinkin' of a master plan" speaks directly to the fact that everything we achieve in the material world is first conceived in the mind. When we pair our thoughts with a plan, we open the door to extraordinary possibilities.

The juxtaposition between the lyrics "So maybe I might just search for a nine to five" and "So I dig into the books of the rhymes that I made ... So now to test to see if I got pull. Hit the studio, 'cuz I'm paid in full" captures the very dilemma entrepreneurs often face: Work for someone else or bet on yourself.

It's the choice between helping someone else fulfill their dream—or digging into your own "books of rhymes" (your ideas, your offerings, your expertise) and making your dream a reality. One day, I knew I was going to be paid in full—full enough to buy a genuine Polo shirt and never wear that knockoff again.

You're Fired!

On Monday, I received a confidential envelope. How did I know it was confidential? Because "CONFIDENTIAL" was stamped in big, bold, red letters across the front.

Inside was a letter from the university provost asking me to meet with him and the university president on Friday. What happened on Friday? You guessed it—I was fired.

I had never been fired from a job in my professional career—well, except that one time I worked at Burger King and they discovered I was 14 and too young to legally work.

But this wasn't that. This was different. I was fired from my *dream job*. I lost my title. I lost my six-figure salary. I lost the health benefits, the perks, and the lifestyle I had been carefully building. But most of all, I lost my pride.

What was I going to do now?
The obvious answer? Find another job. Duh.

Stuck in Park

Back in high school, I used to cruise down the street in my '64.

Okay, that's a line from N.W.A's "Boyz-n-the-Hood." I didn't have a '64 Impala. What I *did* have was a yellow, boxy 1979 Ford Granada, which I lovingly (and laughingly) called the "Yellow Square Banana."

This was pre-iPhone. Pre-texting. But we had PalmPilots and pagers—and we were just as distracted as the young folks are today. One afternoon, sitting at a red light, I looked down at my pager and accidentally bumped the gear shift into park. When the light turned green, I pressed the gas—but the car didn't move. The engine revved, but I went nowhere. Behind me, horns blared. In my rearview mirror, I saw drivers yelling, gesturing, and furious.

That moment became the perfect metaphor for my life post firing.

I thought I'd bounce back quickly. I had the title, the doctorate, the network. Surely, I'd land a new job in six months—if not sooner.

But six months came and went. I participated in more than two dozen interviews across the country—and came back empty-handed every time. No offers. No income. Just a growing pile of rejection letters and "nothing but lint" in my pockets.

The longer the silence, the more I began to question everything. Was I actually good at what I did? Was the VP title a fluke? Had the storm wiped away my entire foundation?

I felt like I was back in the Yellow Banana—foot on the gas, light turned green, engine roaring, and still stuck in park.

All In and Burn the Ships

Then came another rejection, the one that finally pushed me over the edge.

"Dr. Lewis,
Thank you for spending time with the search committee at University X.

The committee has decided not to advance your candidacy for the Vice President of Diversity and Inclusion position. Best wishes in your future endeavors."

As I read the email, my heart pounded. My hands trembled. I wanted this job—needed it. I was ready to move to the West Coast. I was emotionally all in. But, apparently, the committee wasn't.

So, I did what any determined job seeker would do: I asked for feedback.

The recruiter was generous. He said I'd nailed the interview. I was polished. Insightful. Qualified.

"But," he added, "they weren't sure you'd stick around. You sounded too much like … a consultant."

Boom.

He was right. I had been consulting during my job search. And somewhere along the way, I had started to enjoy it—*really* enjoy it.

A few days later, I shared that conversation with my mentor, Glen—a former diversity officer and university president. Glen listened quietly, then said, "Will, here's the problem, man … You're not all in."

He was right again. I was straddling the fence—half in the job market, half in entrepreneurship. Playing both sides, just in case.

And then Glen hit me with the story of Hernán Cortés, and that changed everything.

In 1519, Spanish conquistador Hernán Cortés landed on the shores of what is now Mexico with six hundred men. As the story goes, once they were on land, he ordered his men to burn the ships they arrived on—sending a clear message that there was no turning back. The only way forward was through total commitment (Díaz del Castillo, 1963).

I got the message: Burn the ships.

No more applying for jobs. No more hedging bets. No more "just in case." I was going to go all in. If I wanted the life I envisioned—the freedom, the purpose, the impact— I'd have to commit fully to the entrepreneurial path.

And so I did.

Recruiters kept sending me VP-level job postings. I read them, smiled … and hit delete.

I was done waiting. I was done wondering. I was ready to build.

When the Storm Is the Sign

But here's what I've learned—not just about entrepreneurship but also about leadership in the storm.

Sometimes the most defining moments aren't when we're winning—but when we're *wrecked*. When the title is gone. When the inbox is empty. When the rejection letter says what you feared was true. That's when the real work begins.

Whether you're an entrepreneur, an executive, or a frontline team leader, the storm doesn't just test your character—it *shapes* it. Leadership isn't born in the calm; it's forged in the chaos.

And the ones who last aren't necessarily the most confident or credentialed. They're the ones who decide—despite the fear, despite the setbacks—to go all in.

Eventually, I had to choose: Stay stuck in park, waiting for a break that might never come—or slam the gas and burn the ships behind me.

With some hard-won wisdom, my mentor's push, and a deep-down belief that I was built for more, I finally did what the storm had been asking of me all along.

I stopped waiting.
I stopped dreaming.
I bet on myself.
I burned the ships.
And I've never looked back.

Well until my client pipeline dried up. Here comes another storm! Geesh!

Leadership isn't born in the calm; it's forged in the chaos.

PART 3:

A PERFECT STORM

"WHEN SEVERAL ADVERSITIES COLLIDE, THEY CREATE A PERFECT STORM—NOT TO DESTROY YOU BUT TO REVEAL THE STRENGTH YOU DIDN'T KNOW YOU HAD."

One of my favorite films is *The Perfect Storm*, starring George Clooney and Mark Wahlberg. Based on a true story and the book of the same name, the movie follows a group of brave fishermen who regularly put their lives on the line, facing unpredictable and often brutal conditions at sea. On Halloween of 1991, their worst nightmare unfolds when three powerful weather systems converge in the North Atlantic: a cold front from Canada moving south, a low-pressure system from the Great Lakes pushing eastward, and the remnants of Hurricane Grace sweeping up from the south. The rare collision of these systems produces an intense and deadly storm—what meteorologists later called "the Perfect Storm."

In this section, I reflect on a period in my life when multiple fronts of adversity collided—personally, professionally, and emotionally. While not catastrophic in the physical sense, the impact was traumatic and disorienting. The convergence of those life storms created a cascading effect that shook the foundation of my leadership and my business. This chapter explores what it means to be caught in a perfect storm— and what resilience looks like in the middle of it.

A perfect storm, as I've come to understand it, doesn't just test you—it *trains* you. It reveals your cracks but also your core.

Dancing in the Rain

I wasn't what you'd call an all-star athlete in high school. I dabbled in track and field and eventually landed in the 400 meters—mainly because I wasn't fast enough for the 100. Running track was brutal. I much preferred dancing with my friends John, Steve, Larry, and Big Steve. Any combo of us five made up the Show Boyz. We were basically New Edition—minus the vocals. Had even one of us been able to carry a tune, I might be on tour right now instead of writing this book.

We were a part of a vibrant local dance community, with our sights set on the ultimate prize: winning the StarQuest Competition at the Indiana Black Expo. Think *America's Got Talent*, but all the judges know your mama. We finally won in 1990, but the fire that got us there was lit by a humiliating loss the summer before.

Two weeks before the Expo, there was this huge community event called Soul Fest—barbecue, music, carnival rides, and the semifinals of StarQuest. If you won there, you'd dance on the big stage at the Indianapolis Convention Center in front of thousands of friends, family members, teachers, and audiences of all ages. The night before our semifinal, we should've been resting and visualizing our routine. Instead, we were scrambling. The tape cassette (yes, cassette!) with our mix became tangled, and we tried our best to fix it. If you remember tape cassettes, then you will recall that once a cassette gets tangled and you try to straighten it out, your music is ruined. We argued, patched together a shaky routine, and finally looked at the clock—3 a.m.

Then came the moment: The announcer belted out (in his Michael Buffer voice), "Coming to the stage … theeee Mighty, Mighty Shhhhowww Boyzzzz!" Our mixtape sputtered to life, we hit the stage … and promptly fell apart. Steps forgotten. Collisions mid-routine. Chaos. We abandoned the choreography and each just started doing our own thing. Hot. Flaming. Mess.

The audience winced in collective embarrassment. I don't think they were embarrassed *for* us. I think they were embarrassed to *know* us.

I am not sure if you've ever experienced failure and embarrassment like that, but it is hard to come back from. That failure hurt our souls, and it was the catalyst for a furious refocus and recommitment to doing something special. Two months later, we met Special K, a local DJ who became our coach, sound tech, and drill sergeant. He gave us two rules: Perfect practice makes perfect, and every mistake means we go back to the top. Guess who made the most mistakes? Yep, yours truly. My rhythm is so bad, my wife still doesn't believe I was ever on the dance floor voluntarily. To this day, she must count me in when we hit the dance floor. Even then, I find myself on a different beat than everyone else.

But what I didn't know at seventeen was this: The same discipline and repetition I hated on the dance floor would later become my lifeline as a leader. Special K didn't just coach us to win; he taught us to fail forward—and start again.

"Houston, We Have a Problem!"

Fast-forward thirty years. I'm in Portland, Oregon, selling my first book, *Sweet Potato or Pumpkin Pie: Conversations with My White Friends about Race*. My wife, Latasha, had set up a booth that was a magnet for conference attendees. Books flying off the table. Selfies. Handshakes.

I was floating. Living the author's dream.

Mid-conversation with a reader, my phone buzzed. I excused myself to take the call.

Me: *"Hello, this is William."*

Caller: *"Will, this is [client]. Your survey tool keeps failing. I'm extremely disappointed. You need to fix this."*

Click.

And just like that, the emotional high was punctured like a balloon. One minute, I was basking in accomplishment; the next, I was sinking in panic.

I called my tech officer, and we scrambled to find a stopgap fix. It worked—barely. We thought the issue was isolated, but then another client ran into the same glitch. At that point, I realized: *This isn't a bump in the road; this is a sinkhole.*

I spent $20,000 creating my own proprietary employee engagement survey tool. I had to pivot fast and ditch it altogether in favor of an outside vendor. That was not part of the plan and a tremendous hit to my pocket. After this flub, I literally had nothing but lint in my pockets.

This journey ain't glamorous. It ain't linear. And it sure as hell ain't easy.

The Repo Man

In 2018, I gave an impassioned welcome to twenty-five diversity, equity, and inclusion (DEI) professionals attending a professional development boot camp in Indianapolis that my former business partner and I created. I told them, "You're in the right place. You're needed. And you've got this."

What they didn't know was that *I* was barely holding it together. That morning, my wife called to say my car had been repossessed. I'd poured everything into making that event work—speakers, food, transportation. It barely broke even.

At the airport, my wife picked me up. I got in her car, closed the door, and broke down in tears. I felt like I had failed her. Failed *us*. And yet, after the tears, I did what Special K taught me: I went back to the top.

Negative $4,887.92

It was supposed to be a normal day—well it was Friday, and I'd just gotten paid. I transferred $500 to my assistant for a project. I had $2,500 in my account. I drove to Cam's Coffee for lunch with my wife and team. By the time I parked, I got a notification: My account was *negative* $4,887.92. What in the actual world?!

Turns out a client's check got hung at the bank due to some issues in their finance department. My bank balance didn't just dip—it went scuba diving. Talk about a perfect storm: a bad check, a holiday weekend, and a negative bank account.

As I sat there stunned, Tasha and the crew tried to lighten the mood. Our daughter, Moot, even made me pay for my own drink. I told her, "With what money?! I'm $4,000 in the hole!" Everyone burst out laughing. I didn't. Tasha was like, "Too soon?" I just looked at her!

Later, Tasha saw the stress all over my face and asked how I was feeling. "Like I am drowning," I replied. It reminded me of when I went whitewater rafting at the National Whitewater Center in Charlotte. One moment, we were gliding along peacefully. The next, the raft flipped. I was underwater—gasping for air, disoriented, tossed like a rag doll in the current. I felt like each time I would catch my breath, another wave would come and knock me back under water. That's how I felt in that moment. Yet another storm I had to survive.

I've been humiliated in public. Lost tens of thousands of dollars. Had moments where I questioned my sanity, my strategy, and my worth. But here's what I've learned: Resilience isn't just a character trait—it's a leadership skill. These storms didn't just batter my confidence; they built my capacity. Each collision with adversity sharpened my ability to adapt, to problem-solve under pressure, and to lead when the map was gone and the skies were dark. That's the heart of resilient leadership—not avoiding the storm but learning how to anchor yourself in it and guide others through it.

So, if you find yourself in your own perfect storm—multiple challenges crashing in at once—don't just ask, "Why is this happening?" Ask, "What is this trying to teach me as a leader?" Because the truth is, storms don't just disrupt your life—they develop your leadership.

PART 4:

REBUILDING IN THE RAIN

"YOU CAN'T STOP THE STORM, BUT YOU CAN REBUILD IN THE RAIN."

This section isn't just about survival—it's about *what comes next*. After the thunder rolls, the wind settles, and the rain lingers ... what do you do? You rebuild, not when the sun returns but while the storm still hovers overhead.

This part of my journey is about the messy middle. The moments when I had to move forward without clarity, keep building without full resources, and believe even when belief felt thin. It's about how I rebuilt—in real time, with rain falling, thunder rumbling, and doubt whispering in my ear.

And here's the thing: This isn't just my story. It's yours too. Every leader has their own rainy season. And whether you're leading a business, a team, a movement, or a family—how you rebuild in the rain makes all the difference.

Whenever I find myself stuck—whether it's personally, professionally, or financially—I say to myself, "I am not going to have this same conversation next year." That's my internal rally cry. It jolts me from complaint to action.

Take, for example, the time I had more consulting projects than I could handle. Sounds like a good problem, right? It was—until it wasn't. Because I got so busy *doing the work* that I stopped *marketing the work*. I skipped the conferences where I usually presented and networked, the exact places where future contracts came from. So, when Q4 hit, I was looking around for opportunities like someone showing up to the cookout after the grill's already cold.

Lesson learned. I told myself, "Never again." I committed to presenting at five conferences the following year. And wouldn't you know—it worked. I hit ten. About half of those were paid, and each one brought new leads. I wasn't just getting wet by the rain; I was building something in it.

But let's not pretend grit alone gets you through. Sometimes the climb is real—and steep.

Mt. Mofo

I'll never forget Mt. Mofo.

Now, I don't know if that was the official name of the hill we climbed at Marine Corps Boot Camp in San Diego or just what we called it because of how brutally disrespectful it felt. But "Mofo" fit. It was the final test before we graduated: a thirteen-mile hike over uneven, unforgiving terrain with full gear.

Rewind two years. It was 1988—the summer before my sophomore year of high school. While most kids were thinking about beach trips and backyard basketball, I was headed into major surgery.

For years, I'd struggled with high ankle sprains. I could be walking down the street, minding my business, step on a pebble—and just like that, a sprain. I never broke anything, but the pain was real. It stole weeks from me. Weeks of healing. Weeks of limping. Weeks of sitting out while others played.

It meant no sports. No hiking. No taekwondo. Just watching from the sidelines, again and again.

Eventually, the doctors decided on a corrective surgery. They removed a half inch of bone from each of my heels and inserted metal rods to stabilize them. I was still young, they said. My bones were strong enough. I'd bounce back.

But let me paint the picture for you—this was summer in the '90s. Outside was everything. We didn't have the kind of video games or endless streaming that kids have now. We lived outside—riding bikes, playing basketball, and just walking up and down the neighborhood.

And here I was—two legs in full, knee-high casts.

But I was determined. I refused to let my summer be stolen.

I rolled through the neighborhood on the back of a friend's mini-moped—two casts and all. I went to a Fresh Fest rap concert, stood in the crowd like I was just as free as anyone else. That summer, I may have been bound physically, but my spirit was wild, determined, and unbreakable.

Okay, maybe I was a little miffed when sweat would roll down my legs and it felt like ants were crawling on me—but even that didn't stop me.

Fast-forward to senior year. I was ready to enlist in the U.S. Marine Corps. I had taken the ASVAB. I'd done the physical. I was ready for that next chapter.

Then the letter came.

Denied. Medical disqualification due to my previous surgeries.

Devastated doesn't even begin to describe how I felt. The military wasn't just an option—it was *the* option. I saw myself as a Marine officer, maybe even a general. That was the path I'd chosen for myself, and suddenly, it was gone.

But here's the turning point.

My mom looked me in the eyes and said, "Son, do you still want to serve?"
I said, "Yes, ma'am."

She said, "Okay then. We're going to make it happen."

Let me tell you—when I think of perseverance, I see my mother. Her picture belongs right there in the dictionary next to the word. She rallied. My sister, who was serving in the Air Force at the time, helped. Together, we wrote to our congressman. We explained everything: my dedication to ROTC, my top cadet status, my clean record, my desire to serve.

Weeks later, another letter arrived: "Congratulations. You've been granted a congressional waiver."

Let me tell you—favor is real. That waiver was divine intervention. It was a second chance. It was a "yes" after a devastating "no." And I didn't take it lightly.

Yes, I sprained my ankle again in boot camp—twice, in fact. But I made it. I served my country. I may not have become an officer, but I earned my GI Bill, bought my first home with a VA loan, and built a foundation that would support me for years to come.

And here's the real point: You can't avoid the storm. You can't go around it. You can't skip over it. You have to walk through it.

That first "no" you hear in life? That's just the rain. That's the wind. That's the thunder rolling. But keep going. Keep showing up. Keep believing.

Because on the other side of the storm … is your breakthrough.

At nineteen, I was in the best shape of my life—and, still, halfway through that climb, I was questioning everything. My legs were shot. My back ached. My willpower was running on fumes. Our drill instructor saw it in our faces and called out: "Boys, do you know how you're going to make it up this mountain?"

We shouted, "Sir, no, sir!"

He said, "PUT YOUR HEAD DOWN AND KEEP YOUR FEET MOVING! Don't give the F' up."

That stuck with me—because it was that type of determination and rebuilding in the rain that allowed me to be on that mountain in the first place.

Leadership is a lot like climbing Mt. Mofo. You're carrying weight other people can't see. You're exhausted, and the goal still looks miles away. And sometimes, the only strategy that works is simple but powerful: Put your head down and keep moving.

And yet—even when you're climbing with everything you've got—life has a way of switching things up. Sometimes the storm isn't just uphill.

Sometimes it hits from the side and demands a pivot.

The COVID Pivot

Remember those line dances—"Cupid Shuffle," "Boot Scootin' Boogie," "Cha-Cha Slide"—where the whole room pivots on cue? That's exactly what March 2020 felt like. One big "turn to the left!" moment—but without the music or the joy.

At the time, my company was poised for its best year ever. Then COVID hit. In a matter of days, every contract on the books vanished. *Poof.*

The storm didn't just show up—it camped out.

So, I did what any entrepreneur in a panic would do: I sat down, cleared the fog in my brain, and "thought of a master plan."

Our bread and butter had been live, in-person events. That was obviously out. But instead of freezing up, my business partner and I reached out to our media collaborator. We got scrappy. We launched a free Zoom webcast series to support higher education professionals trying to navigate DEI work in a virtual world. (Side note: If I had invested in Zoom stock in March 2020, this chapter might've been written from a beach in Bali.)

Those webcasts turned out to be more than a survival strategy—they became our pivot. Our email list grew *tenfold*. We created and launched an online learning academy that brought in $18,000 in thirty days.

The key wasn't perfection—it was movement. It was staying present, visible, and relevant, even when it felt easier to wait for the world to right itself. That pivot reminded me of another lesson I keep returning to: Not every swing will land, but you keep swinging.

Swing for the PING

Golf is humbling. Especially when you swing like me.

In my mind, I look like Tiger Woods—smooth stroke, perfect aim, pro-level form. In reality? Let's just say it's not pretty. But every now and then, something magic happens. I make perfect contact, and I hear it: *PING*. That sound—the crisp, clean PING of club meeting ball—is everything.

It doesn't happen often, but it happens just enough to keep me coming back. That one PING makes the other ninety-nine misses worth it.

My first taste of that entrepreneurial PING came in 1999. I had just finished my master's in social work, thought I was ready to bless the world with all I knew about systems theory and cultural competency. I printed flyers, rented space at the YWCA, and prepared for twenty-five participants. I got one. *One.* And two other folks who wandered in looking for their kids. But that one paying participant? They were my PING.

Fast-forward twenty years: My business partner and I hosted a higher-ed leadership conference that made nearly $60,000.

Then in 2025, I teamed up with Roderick Lewis (no relation, but family nonetheless) to host the Belonging and Inclusion Leadership Summit at Wake Forest University. One hundred and forty registrants. Six sponsors. $20,000 raised and an enlightened community.

From one attendee at the YWCA to two successful leadership conferences—that's the PING, y'all.

But even that success didn't come from faith alone.

Faith and Action

I'll never forget a TikTok Tasha sent me: A contractor was venting about a failed home sale. The buyer claimed they'd pay cash from a generous gift from their father. But when closing day came, no cash. Why? The buyer said their Heavenly Father hadn't given it to them yet.

Friends, I'm a man of faith. But that was next-level faith … or next-level foolishness, depending on how you frame it. I absolutely believe in God's provision. But I also believe in matching faith with action. As the Bible says: "Thus also faith by itself, if it does not have works, is dead" (The Holy Bible, New King James Version, 1982, James 2:17).

And Hebrews reminds us: "Now faith is the substance of things hoped for, the evidence of things not seen" (The Holy Bible, New King James Version, 1982, Hebrews 11:1).

This book you're holding? It's faith and action in real time. When I wrote *Sweet Potato or Pumpkin Pie*, my business was booming—I had the means to publish. But this book? At the time I started writing, my pipeline was a trickle, and my bank account was limping along.

Still, I believed God would provide. I held on to my faith. Not blindly but boldly. And that faith moved me to write, edit, and push forward. Because faith isn't magic. It's movement.

The story of the woman and the oil from 2 Kings 4:1–7 comes to mind. The woman's husband had died, and the creditors were coming for her stuff. She didn't have the money to pay the collection agencies. (I've been there.) With nothing but a jar of oil in her cabinet, the woman went to the prophet Elisha and asked him for help. The prophet told her to gather her jar and go to her neighbors and ask for their jars. Once she gathered the jars, the prophet instructed her to pour her own oil into the gathered jars. She didn't question the prophet. She moved. She gathered. She poured.

And she was blessed beyond measure. She ended up with enough jars of oil that she was able to pay the bill collectors and have enough to live on (The Holy Bible, New King James Version, 1982, 2 Kings 4:1–7).

Likewise, I didn't have much when I started writing this project—just stories, conviction, and a little creative oil. But I poured it anyway, and God did the rest. And here we are. The divine manifestation of my faith and action is in your hands.

You Rebuild in the Rain

Whether it's drying out from a tough Q4, dragging yourself up Mt. Mofo, pivoting in a pandemic, chasing the elusive PING, or trusting God even when the budget doesn't balance—here's the truth: You can't wait for the storm to pass. You've got to rebuild in the rain. You've got to rebuild drenched and inconvenienced.

You move. You pivot. You swing. You believe. You pour.

Leadership isn't about perfection. It's about perseverance. You don't need to have it all figured out. You just need to take the next step. And then the next. And then the next.

Put your head down.
Keep your feet moving.
Keep swinging for the PING.
Keep pouring what you have.
And trust God—the breakthrough is already on the way.

SECTION
TWO

PART 5:

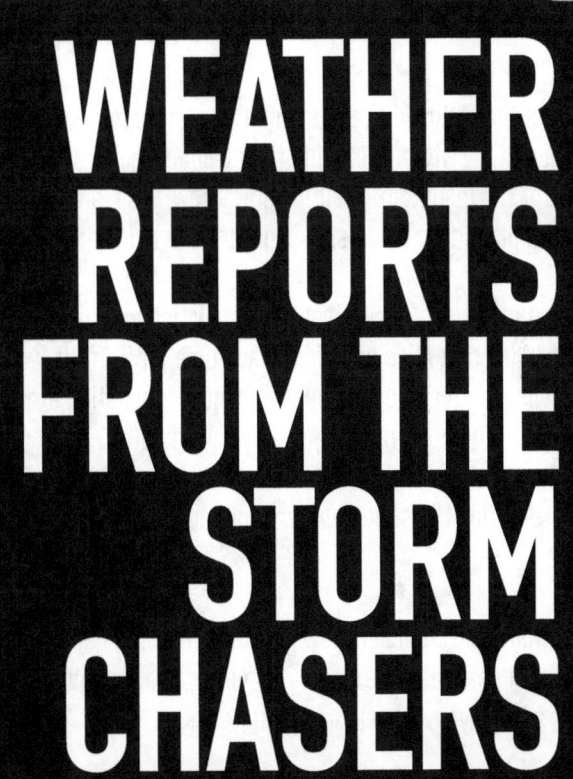

WEATHER REPORTS FROM THE STORM CHASERS

"SOME PEOPLE CHASE THE SUN. ENTREPRENEURS CHASE STORMS—AND LEARN TO BUILD IN THEM."

This section is a collection of real-world reports—dispatches from the front lines of entrepreneurship. These are conversations with founders, builders, side-hustlers, and folks who support entrepreneurs from the sidelines. The goal? To show you that storms are universal. But so is the grit it takes to withstand them—and, more importantly, to build in the middle of them.

Because here's the truth: You can't summit your entrepreneurial or leadership journey without learning from people who've already climbed part of the mountain. Their insights—raw, wise, and often hilarious—remind us that leadership is never done in isolation.

When I started my own journey, I was blessed with a mentor named Bill. Bill was in his seventies and didn't have time for fluff. He was the kind of man who could call a college president, a foundation executive, or a board chair—and get a meeting just by saying hello.

Bill had one rule: Don't mistake *moments* of success for a *life* of success.

"You gave a great speech? Cool. Now give ten more. You had a good year? Do it again next year," he'd say. "Repeat it. Show me consistency. Then maybe, just maybe, I'll celebrate you."

Whew. Bill didn't hand out gold stars. But he did hand out golden wisdom. One of the best things he taught me was that your network is just as important as your work. And I'm still building mine every day.

Hopefully *you* will become a part of my network!

Curious by nature (and a pretty cool cat, if I may say so), I wanted to hear what advice other entrepreneurs had received from their mentors. So, I took to Facebook and asked a simple question: *What's the best piece of entrepreneurial advice you've ever received?*

Here's a sampling of the responses:

"Do it scared."

"Don't get distracted by what others are doing. Trust God and trust the process."

"Write it down. Meditate. Pray."

"Study others—learn from both their wins and mistakes."

"Stay in your lane."

"Don't let fear block your greatness."

"Have a care team."

"Do the self-work. That's the foundation of legacy."

"Sometimes failure is just faith being tested."

"Build your team—lawyer, accountant, advisors."

"Success takes time. Be prepared for anything."

"You miss 100 percent of the shots you don't take."

Some of these nuggets felt like mic drops. Others, like full-on weather alerts: *Storm's coming. Brace yourself.*

Still curious, I went a step further. I reached out to a few entrepreneurial friends to hear their stories firsthand. I wanted to know not just what they *did* but what they *felt*—what kept them going when the skies turned dark.

You'll find their full stories in the next section, lightly edited for grammar and clarity. What you'll notice quickly is that these aren't all millionaires or startup darlings.

Some are veterans with thirty years in the game. Some are just getting started. Some haven't owned businesses themselves but support founders as advisors, funders, and champions.

They're from all walks of life—middle class, working class, wealthy; Black, White; boomers, Gen Xers, and millennials; first-gen college grads and PhDs; women and men.

But they all have one thing in common: They've been through some storms—and they've got some crazy stories to prove it.

Because storms don't discriminate—but they do refine. And these stories? They're living proof that resilience, paired with bold action and a little divine wind at your back, can carry you farther than you ever imagined.

To help you get the most out of these weather reports, try this:

Storm-Tracking Assignment

Listen for the emotional forecast.

- Grab a pen, your phone, or a napkin from your kitchen table and jot down what emotions you hear in their voices. Have you felt those same winds—fear, frustration, hope, pride?
- Track the leadership lessons. Reflect on the moments that resonate. Then ask:
    - ▷ What keeps *you* going when the storm clouds roll in?
    - ▷ What would you tell your younger self about stepping into the unknown?
    - ▷ What's one lesson from entrepreneurship you can apply in your workplace or team?

So, grab your umbrella—and your journal. The forecast ahead is real talk, high winds, and clear insight.

Let's head into the storm together.

"ALTHOUGH THIS BUSINESS OWNERSHIP JOURNEY CAN BE HARD, I HAVE BEEN ABLE TO DO SOME AMAZING THINGS—THINGS I OTHERWISE WOULDN'T HAVE ATTEMPTED. THINGS I DIDN'T KNOW HOW TO DO, AND THINGS I DIDN'T HAVE THE COURAGE TO TRY."

– FABI PRESLAR

Storm Chaser:
Fabi Preslar, SPARK Publications

Fabi Preslar is a good friend of mine. She is the founder and president of SPARK Publications, a custom publisher of independently published books, magazines, and catalogs. She is the publisher of this book and of my first book, *Sweet Potato or Pumpkin Pie: Conversations with My White Friends about Race*.

Fabi's firm publishes nonfiction entrepreneurial books—business books, coffee table books, cookbooks, workbooks. Their magazines serve large national business-to-business and association markets, helping grow business and memberships. At the heart of their work is a clear mission: to help successful leaders and business owners amplify their platforms.

SPARK Publications is celebrating twenty-eight years in business. Fabi has the unique privilege of working with her husband of thirty-eight years, their daughter, and a deeply talented crew of SPARKlers. She has been named one of the 100 Women to KNOW in America, inducted into the North Carolina Women Business Owners Hall of Fame, and was recognized as National Association of Women Business Owners Charlotte's Woman Business Owner of the Year. Her firm has earned more than 350 industry awards for client work.

Below is my conversation with Fabi, edited for clarity and flow.

Will: *Twice this week, I found myself singing your praises. I was talking to a colleague and suggested she write a book. It's advice I give to anyone who will listen—I believe everyone has at least one book inside of them. For her, it's especially important, as she's transitioning from employee to entrepreneur. A book can quickly establish credibility beyond her PhD. There's a mystique about being an author. The book doesn't have to be extensive; it just has to offer value. She asked if I had an editor, and I told her I have something better: a publisher. When she's ready, I'll introduce her to you!*

Fabi: *Awesome. Thank you for keeping me in mind and helping your colleague. That's fantastic.*

Will: *Absolutely. Let's dive into this interview. What is your why? Why did you start your business?*

Fabi: *My biggest why was personal and family growth. I was managing other people's businesses, and it left me with less and less time for my daughter. I wanted to be present for her. Professionally, I had a mix of skills that didn't fit neatly into any one role. I had already owned a business once before, went back to corporate for a bit, and then started this one cold turkey. I wouldn't advise that!*

Will: *What was your previous business?*

Fabi: *A graphic and marketing design company with a partner. I had the chance to work with a printer in the 1980s—around the time Hurricane Hugo hit. I ended up helping build a new publishing company. But I made the mistake of sharing a lawyer with my partner. The paperwork essentially made me an employee rather than an owner. I was released from the business I helped start.*

Will: *Wow. You got kicked out of your own company?*

Fabi: *Yep. I didn't know my legal rights. That was a tough lesson.*

Will: *I can relate! I've had a business partnership end like a bad divorce.*

Fabi: *Exactly. You need a plan for the end even before the beginning.*

Will: *Let's shift to SPARK Publications. What is it, who do you serve, and how did you get started?*

Fabi: *We're an independent custom publishing firm. We design and produce magazines for large national associations and publish books for entrepreneurial leaders, typically business owners ready to expand their reach. We consult, design, and manage the full publishing process.*

Will: *I remember our first conversation. You asked if I had a book in me. I didn't know where to begin, but you gave me the confidence to get started. Now I'm part of the SPARK family.*

Fabi: *Yes, yes.*

Will: *You mentioned starting your business cold turkey. What did you mean?*

Fabi: *I didn't build systems or do client outreach in advance. I had a name and a vision but no foundation. I just waited for the phone to ring—and it didn't. It was 1998. I started writing letters and introducing myself. Looking back, I should have started as a side hustle.*

Will: *That had to be challenging.*

Fabi: *It was. But it also forced me to figure things out fast. I had no choice but to make it work.*

Will: *Twenty-eight years later, what's your secret?*

Fabi: *It's the impact. Seeing our work help clients grow keeps me going. Even when I've wanted to quit, the next client or project shows me why I started.*

Will: *What business failure taught you the most?*
Fabi: *Hiring. I wanted to save the world and people but learned you have to hire for alignment. Having the right mindset and team is everything.*

Will: *Let's talk work–life balance and working with your spouse. How do you manage it?*
Fabi: *I don't believe in work–life balance. It's all one life. My husband needs separation, so we set boundaries. Working with our daughter has also been a blessing. We complement each other well.*

Will: *What's made business easier for you?*
Fabi: *Clear boundaries and a service mindset. We define what we do and don't do. That keeps us from burning out.*

Will: *What emotions come with the highs and lows?*
Fabi: *Whiplash. Some days are magical; others are a mess. But I've learned not to take it personally. Emotional regulation is everything. Fear blocks creativity.*

Will: *What keeps you going when you want to quit?*
Fabi: *I remind myself: It won't be easier somewhere else. I built this. It's mine. And I have control over its future.*

Will: *Last question, how important is a growth mindset, especially in leadership roles?*
Fabi: *You have to mourn the old vision sometimes to fully embrace the new one. We shifted to remote work during the pandemic. That was huge for us.*

Will: *Fabi, thank you for sharing your wisdom. This was rich!*
Fabi: *Thank you for the opportunity, Will.*

My conversation with Fabi was an inspiring deep dive into the realities of entrepreneurship, resilience, and purpose-driven leadership. From her early struggles in business partnerships to the creation of SPARK Publications, Fabi's journey reflects the importance of perseverance, strategic pivots, and unwavering belief in one's work.

A central theme of our discussion was the power of authorship in establishing credibility and impact. Fabi's work has helped many entrepreneurial leaders turn their expertise into lasting, tangible assets through books and magazines that elevate their brands. She also reinforced a key lesson of business ownership—the necessity of clear agreements and legal protections to safeguard one's contributions and vision.

Fabi's longevity in business is a testament to the value of service, both to her clients and to the team she has built. Her insight on the emotional roller coaster of business ownership—learning to celebrate wins, process losses quickly, and stay focused on the future—offers valuable guidance for any entrepreneur. She also provided wisdom on integrating work and life rather than seeking an unattainable balance, especially when working alongside family.

At the core of every entrepreneurial journey lies a universal truth: **Being a leader means learning how to stand in the storm.**

Storm Chasers like Fabi don't run from the dark clouds—they scan the skies, brace for impact, and keep moving forward with purpose. They don't just weather the storm; they learn from it, build through it, and emerge stronger on the other side.

Fabi's story left me with a few standout takeaways for anyone leading through storms.

Personal and Professional Growth Are Intertwined

- Leadership isn't just about professional success; it's about aligning work with personal values and lifestyle choices.
- Leaders should evaluate whether their roles allow them to maintain a balance between career and personal fulfillment.

Strategic Career Growth Requires Intentionality

- Building credibility through thought leadership (such as by writing a book, publishing articles, or participating in speaking engagements) can elevate professional status and open new opportunities.
- Employees transitioning into leadership roles should be proactive in shaping their own career trajectory rather than waiting for opportunities to appear.

Success Requires Adaptability and the Ability to Pivot

- Businesses and leadership roles require flexibility to effectively navigate change.
- Leaders should regularly assess their strategies and be willing to pivot in response to industry shifts, technological advancements, and evolving team needs.

Employee Growth and Team Dynamics Matter

- Hiring and retaining the right team members is crucial.
- Leaders should shift their mindset from "saving" struggling employees to hiring and developing the right talent that aligns with organizational goals.

Service-Oriented Leadership Drives Success

- Focusing on service—whether to clients, employees, or the broader organization—leads to long-term success.
- Leaders should clarify their core mission and align their strategies around effectively serving their teams and stakeholders.

Fabi's journey reminds us that **the storm doesn't just shake you, it shapes you.** And if you can ride out the winds with wisdom and courage, you just might come out stronger—and with a story worth publishing.

Fabi's story offers valuable insight—but the real transformation begins when you apply these lessons to your own storm. Now it's your turn to step into the storm and reflect.

Storm-Tracking Assignment

- What storms have tested your vision?
- How do you recover after professional disappointment?
- Who or what reminds you why you do what you do?
- Are you building boundaries that protect your purpose?

"IMAGINATION IS THE INGREDIENT TO SUCCESS. EVERY MAJOR INNOVATION—FROM THE TELEPHONE TO ELECTRICITY—STARTED AS AN IDEA IN SOMEONE'S MIND."

– ROD BROWN

Rod Brown, CEO of Greenwood Logistic Solutions, LLC

Rod Brown is the CEO of Greenwood Logistic Solutions, LLC, a game-changing transportation company set to revolutionize the industry with its innovative solutions. He is also a certified coach, passionate educator, and serial entrepreneur with over twenty-five years of experience launching and scaling successful businesses.

In addition to Greenwood, Rod serves as CEO of SouthSide United Health Centers, a medical practice company based in Winston-Salem. He cofounded OnceLogix, LLC, the company behind ShareNote.com, a leading web-based tool for the behavioral health sector. OnceLogix achieved a successful exit in 2022. He also cofounded The Small Business Cookout, a platform that advances minority- and women-owned businesses. Rod's work has earned him recognition on the Inc. 5000 and Forbes Small Giants lists.

His mission is to disrupt traditional systems and create value for customers, partners, and the community.

To my family, Rod is a mentor, investor, and friend.

Below is my conversation with Rod, edited for clarity and flow.

Will: *Rod, one of the things I admire about you is your focus on mindset. You consistently promote a positive and entrepreneurial mindset. Your social media posts often challenge people to nurture a growth mindset and think differently. How important is it to have an entrepreneurial mindset?*

Rod: *Mindset is crucial—not just for entrepreneurship but for life. The way you think affects everything. On a micro level, it impacts how you start your morning and carry yourself throughout the day. On a macro level, it shapes your trajectory. If you want a lifestyle business, your mindset must match that. If you're aiming for generational wealth or building an enterprise, your actions, risk tolerance, and discipline must align with that goal. Once your mind is fixed on your destination, your behaviors will follow.*

Will: *How do you develop that kind of mindset?*

Rod: *It starts with who you surround yourself with. I also took time to understand how the brain works. About 95 percent of the 80,000 thoughts we have daily are negative—it's a survival mechanism. So, you can't just "stop" thinking negatively, but you can train your mind. For me, that means daily meditation, intentional self-talk, and recalling past successes to build confidence. I practice emotional intelligence. I don't let emotions run me. I acknowledge them, process them, and move on.*

Will: *That's why I love talking to you, man. You go deep. I know you're also a big reader. How often do you read?*

Rod: *I aim to tap into a new book or two each month. I use audiobooks a lot since I'm in the car. Books are like a portable mastermind. Even if a book covers familiar ground, there's often one paragraph that can shift your entire perspective. I'm always looking for those nuggets of wisdom.*

Will: *Let's talk about imagination. I listen to Billy Alsbrook, a motivational speaker on YouTube. He says, "Success comes off the assembly line of my mind." How important is imagination for an entrepreneur?*

Rod: *Imagination is everything. Think of a child learning without formal language. They imagine how the world works, and that imagination helps them adapt and grow. Innovation happens the same way. Alexander Graham Bell and Lewis Latimer imagined talking to someone who wasn't there. Edison imagined lighting up a room without fire. You have to be willing to throw ideas at the wall. Something will stick.*

Will: *Tell me about a time in business when you failed. What were your emotions?*

Rod: *I don't think people are failures. You can fail, but you're not a failure unless you quit. I've had repossessions, home foreclosures, and even bankruptcy. Those things hurt. I remember sitting in a bankruptcy orientation and seeing someone I knew—embarrassing. But it made me stronger. I learned, recovered, and moved forward. Failures build calluses. They make you storm-ready.*

Will: *You've worked with partners. What have you learned about business partnerships?*

Rod: *Partnerships are like marriages. You need trust, communication, and clear expectations. Know your lane, stay in it, and check your ego. Define responsibilities early and revisit them often.*

Will: *How do you manage work–life balance?*

Rod: *I don't believe in traditional balance. It depends on the business you want. If you own a job or want a lifestyle business, balance is more achievable. But if you're building an enterprise, the business comes first. Sacrifice is part of the journey.*

Will: *Okay, man. Thank you for sharing your thoughts with me. I appreciate you.*

My conversation with Rod Brown was a masterclass in mindset, resilience, and strategic thinking. As a seasoned entrepreneur, investor, and leader, Rod emphasized that success begins with how you think. A strong mindset doesn't just impact your morning routine—it defines your long-term vision, your ability to navigate failure, and your willingness to lead with integrity.

Rod is the embodiment of a **Storm Chaser**. He doesn't shy away from turbulence—he studies it, learns from it, and steps into it with purpose. His reflections on imagination reminded me that innovation doesn't start with capital; it starts with creativity. His perspective on failure—that you're not a failure unless you quit—is powerful. He shared this perspective with our family when we were forced to close the doors of our coffee shop during COVID. We didn't quit; we pivoted and opened an online coffee store. His advice helped us make that pivot.

His transparency about financial loss and emotional recovery brings necessary authenticity to conversations about success.

And while Rod's insights speak clearly to entrepreneurs, his lessons apply to anyone in leadership. Whether you're scaling a business, leading a team, or managing change, the principles remain the same: Sharpen your mindset, regulate your emotions, build trust in your relationships, and don't be afraid to dream big.

Rod's story left me with a few standout takeaways for anyone leading through storms.

Mindset Is the Foundation of Success

- A leader's mindset affects their daily performance, decision-making, and long-term career growth.
- Align your actions with your aspirations—whether that's stability, influence, or enterprise-level impact.
- Embrace challenges as growth opportunities.

Emotional Intelligence Is Key to Leadership

- Regulate emotions rather than react impulsively.
- Replace negative thoughts with intentional affirmations.
- Emotional control supports clarity and consistency under pressure.

Continuous Learning Is a Leadership Advantage

- Reading and reflection offer constant access to new strategies.
- Leaders who learn consistently adapt faster and lead better.
- Books are your silent mentors—use them.

Imagination Fuels Innovation

- Dreaming up new ideas is the starting point of innovation.
- Encourage creative thinking across your team.
- Don't dismiss big ideas because they're untested.

Failure Is a Lesson, Not an Identity

- Everyone fails. Growth happens in the response.
- Use failures to build mental strength and clarity.
- You're not a failure unless you quit.

Work–Life Balance Is About Prioritization

- Define what matters to you at each stage of life and leadership.
- Be honest about what your ambitions require.
- Set boundaries that serve your goals—not someone else's expectations.
- Rod's story offers valuable insight—but the real transformation begins when you apply these lessons to your own storm. Now it's your turn to step into the storm and reflect.

Storm-Tracking Assignment

- What area of your mindset needs a reset to match your leadership goals?
- When have you faced failure, and how did you bounce back?
- Are you building relationships with trust and clearly defined roles?
- Where do you need to give your imagination more room to lead?

"I REALIZED I DIDN'T HAVE TO WAIT UNTIL I WAS SIXTY-FIVE TO START LIVING THE LIFE I WANTED. I BUILT MY CAREER AROUND MY FREEDOM, NOT THE OTHER WAY AROUND. NOW, MY OFFICE IS WHEREVER I CHOOSE, MY SCHEDULE ALIGNS WITH MY ENERGY, AND MY SUCCESS IS MEASURED BY HOW MUCH JOY AND CREATIVITY I CAN INFUSE INTO MY DAYS. LIVING ON MY OWN TERMS ISN'T A DREAM—IT'S A DECISION."

— STARLIGHT MUNDY

Starlight Mundy, Bottled Lightning

Starlight (yes, really) is the creator of Bottled Lightning, a growth strategy consultancy. She spent the early years of her career immersed in user experience, human-centered program design, and technology—primarily in the startup and innovation scenes. (Her patented inventions are in your phone and on your smart TV right now.)

Today, she helps thought leaders and experts (I am one of her clients) around the globe unleash transformative thinking. When she's not traveling to facilitate training and speaking, she's doing deep work at a beachside café, chillin' with her dog, or salsa dancing on a floating bar.

Below is my conversation with Starlight, edited for clarity and flow.

Will: *Starlight, from what I know about you, you wanted to live life on your own terms and decided to live and work in a vacation destination.*
Starlight: *Yeah, yeah. Right!*

Will: *Let's dig into that. As an entrepreneur, depending on your work, you're not tied to a nine-to-five schedule or a physical office. What does your workday look like, and where do you work from?*
Starlight: *It depends on where my clients are. Right now, I'm serving a lot of people in the UK, so I've become a bit of a*

morning person. I walk, have breakfast, then sit at my desk early. When I had more West Coast clients, I could sleep in and work late. That's the real freedom for me—adjusting my schedule based on what works now. I can prioritize the things I love, like beach time with my dog and quality time with friends, without compromising my work.

Will: *What made you leave the States?*
Starlight: *When I left corporate, I was based in San Diego—close to the beach but still drowning in rent and traffic. Eventually, I realized I could meet clients virtually. That sparked the idea: What if I did this from somewhere better? I downsized, packed up, and relocated.*
Time zones were the only real consideration. I needed to be close enough to serve my clients. I ended up in Bocas del Toro, Panama—no traffic, lower costs, slower pace, and still profitable. It's been seven years.

Will: *Wow! Seven years ago you said, "To hell with this, I'm out. I'm going to live life on my own terms."*
Starlight: *Ha! Pretty much. But the idea started about twelve years ago. I met some retired snowbirds in Mexico and realized, "Why wait until I'm sixty-five?" With my skills, I could make this lifestyle work now. That realization set everything in motion.*

Will: *Talk to me about work–life balance.*
Starlight: *I used to be terrible at it—workaholic level. Gabor Maté's work on socially acceptable addictions like overworking opened my eyes. I was burned out. Balance for me now is about boundaries. I think of life like three pots on a stove: work, self-care, and life. Balance is keeping each pot from boiling over. Sometimes emergencies shift priorities, but I try to keep the burners steady.*

Will: *That's a strong image. How important is imagination in your work?*

Starlight: *It's everything. People think imagination is a talent— it's a skill. I'm known for "Starlight ideas" because I've trained myself to think beyond the obvious. Like the Queen of Hearts says in* Through the Looking-Glass, *"I think of six impossible things before breakfast."*
Good imagination is tied to good problem-solving. You have to slow down, explore the problem deeply before rushing to solve it. That's how better ideas emerge.

Will: *That's great advice for both entrepreneurs and intrapreneurs. What about failure—tell me about a tough moment and what it taught you.*

Starlight: *Early in my career, I worked for a high-pressure startup. They brought in Brian Tracy, and I remember him saying, "Failure isn't quitting—it's knowing when to quit." That stuck with me. In our think tank, we constantly had to vet and scrap ideas that didn't work. It taught me to detach emotionally from failure. If it's not working, move on. That perspective has helped me grow faster and waste less energy.*

Will: *So, when you let go, you're not giving up—you're freeing up space for what's next.*

Starlight: *Exactly. There've been tears and frustration, but I've learned to pause, reflect, and pivot. That's how I stay creative and resilient.*

Will: *That's a powerful insight. Thank you, Starlight.*

Starlight's journey embodies the essence of living and leading on one's own terms, demonstrating how intentional decision-making, imagination, and adaptability can lead to both personal fulfillment and professional success.

Her story highlights the importance of flexibility and strategic independence. She transitioned from a high-stress corporate life to running a successful consulting business from a Caribbean island, proving that work can be structured around lifestyle goals rather than the other way around. By leveraging remote work, she reduced stressors like long commutes and high costs while maintaining a thriving career.

As a **Storm Chaser**, Starlight didn't just run from the pressure—she redefined the environment. Her success wasn't born from following traditional rules but from rewriting them. Her story reminds us that creativity, courage, and clarity can be powerful tools in any leader's toolkit—no matter the industry or location.

One of the biggest takeaways is her approach to imagination. Starlight views creativity not as an innate gift but as a skill leaders must develop. She encourages slowing down, exploring problems deeply, and creating space for new thinking— essential practices for innovation and strategic leadership.

Her honest reflections on burnout, boundaries, and failure offer refreshing insight into the realities of modern leadership. Instead of chasing an unrealistic idea of balance, she manages energy across the domains of work, life, and self-care—and gives herself grace when priorities shift. Her perspective on failure is liberating: Success doesn't mean seeing every idea through; it means knowing when to pivot and move forward.

Ultimately, Starlight's journey is a call to live and lead with intention. Whether you're an entrepreneur or a corporate leader, the message is clear: Design your career with purpose, build habits that nurture creativity, and lead with enough flexibility to respond to change—without losing sight of joy.

Starlight's story left me with a few standout takeaways for anyone leading through storms.

Work–Life Balance Is About Boundaries, Not Perfection

- Set clear work boundaries to prevent burnout.
- Prioritize self-care and personal time alongside professional responsibilities.
- Accept that balance isn't always perfect—some areas will require more focus at different times.

Cultivating Imagination Enhances Leadership and Problem-Solving

- Imagination can be developed as a skill.
- Foster creative problem-solving by
    - ▷ spending more time understanding problems before jumping to solutions,
    - ▷ encouraging teams to think beyond traditional answers, and
    - ▷ creating a workplace culture where new ideas are valued and explored.

Knowing When to Pivot Is a Leadership Strength

- "Failure isn't quitting; it's knowing when to quit."
- Let go of ineffective strategies and move forward with new approaches.
- Identify when a project, process, or mindset is no longer serving the team or company.
- Help teams see failure as a natural part of innovation.

Flexibility in Work Styles Can Increase Productivity

- Empower employees with flexible work arrangements.
- Be open to remote, hybrid, and asynchronous work structures.
- Focus on results, not just hours worked.

Success Is About Intentional Living and Leadership

- Define career goals based on what matters most.
- Support career development aligned with passion and purpose.
- Encourage ownership, creativity, and reflection within your team.

Starlight's story offers valuable insight—but the real transformation begins when you apply these lessons to your own storm. Now it's your turn to step into the storm and reflect.

Storm-Tracking Assignment

- Are your current boundaries protecting your well-being—or blurring it?
- Where could your imagination lead to more creative problem-solving at work?
- What's one area where you may need to pivot rather than push through?
- How intentionally are you designing your career—and your life?

"I DIDN'T KNOW ANYTHING ABOUT RUNNING A BUSINESS AT FIRST, AND I HAD TO LEARN THE HARD WAY—LOTS OF TEARS, TRIAL AND ERROR, AND SOME TOUGH LESSONS ABOUT TRUST. BUT THROUGH IT ALL, I KEPT GOING. NOW, I ABSOLUTELY FEEL LIKE AN ENTREPRENEUR."

– TA'NISHA MONIQUE

Ta'Nisha Monique, The Sifted Sugar, Inc.

Ta'Nisha Monique began baking as a way to cope with the loss of her grandmother in 2012, while still working in corporate America. What started as therapeutic baking evolved into a thriving business. In 2018, the business outgrew her personal kitchen, prompting her to open a storefront bakery. Since then, she's served customers across the country—including Ella Mai, Angela Rye, and Tahiry Jose.

Despite the loss that launched her journey, she now lives one of her dreams—baking full-time alongside her mother and daughter. That's three generations of bakers! Every dessert includes custom recipes and personalized designs. At Ta'Nisha Monique Cupcakes, the vision really is edible.

She's not only a fellow entrepreneur; she's a trusted friend of our family business, Cam's Coffee Co.

Below is our conversation, edited for clarity and flow.

Will: *Ta'Nisha, there's a book called* The E-Myth *that talks about how people who are great at a craft—like baking—often get pushed into business. But once they're in, they realize the business side is a different beast. Did that happen to you? Were you a practitioner who became an entrepreneur, or did you always plan to run a business?*

Ta'Nisha: *I was definitely thrown into it. I always loved baking. I'd do it with my mom and grandma, and then baking shows got popular—everyone thought they could bake. I baked for fun and brought cupcakes to my job in corporate America.*

My coworkers loved them. One even started a Facebook page for me. When I brought cupcakes to work, they'd sell out before I got to my desk. Then Blue Cross had a big layoff. I got laid off, and my dad said, "Go all in on baking." We made a deal to see if my cupcakes or his service station would take off. The station is gone. I'm still baking.

Will: *So, baking started as a hobby. Losing your job pushed you into business. What was it like learning entrepreneurship?*

Ta'Nisha: *It was rough—so many tears and mistakes. One of the first hard lessons? A friend bought up all my domain names after I told him about my business. I had to pay thousands to get them back. I didn't even know that was something to worry about. I leaned on other business owners and went to workshops at Forsyth Tech. The community really helped.*

Will: *That's a brutal lesson. How did that affect your trust in people?*

Ta'Nisha: *I was angry and hurt. I realized not everyone wants to see you win. That situation showed me who I could trust— and who I had to leave behind. Most of the people I opened the bakery with aren't around anymore.*

Will: *Let's talk about another major challenge—the break-in. What happened?*

Ta'Nisha: *Someone broke in and stole a cell phone. A friend ended up buying that phone and told me about it. The community showed up big time. Candace Benbow started the hashtag "#BuyOutOurBakery," and we raised $30,000 in one day. I didn't even have insurance at the time. Another hard lesson.*

Will: *And they weren't stealing cupcakes, right?*
Ta'Nisha: *Nope—just someone on drugs looking for quick cash. The bakery is in an underserved area. I've got insurance now and learned to secure everything.*

Will: *After everything, do you now feel like a true entrepreneur?*
Ta'Nisha: *Absolutely. No question.*

Will: *Let's talk about the cooking shows—how did that happen?*
Ta'Nisha: *Social media. I posted consistently and they found me. First was* Sugar Rush Christmas *on Netflix. I thought it was a scam! My original partner backed out, and the replacement didn't work out great.*

Will: *What about the second show?*
Ta'Nisha: Buddy vs. Duff *on Food Network. During COVID, it was a virtual panel. We judged the chefs through Zoom.*

Will: *Tasha told me you didn't sift the sugar on* Sugar Rush *and that it inspired a name change. What's the story?*
Ta'Nisha: *Yep! I forgot to sift the sugar and got eliminated. I turned that into something positive. I renamed the business "Sifted Sugar" as a play on that mistake—a reminder that the business journey itself isn't a mistake.*

Will: *What was the business name before?*
Ta'Nisha: *Ta'Nisha Monique Cupcakes. People came in expecting to see me every time. That tied me to the store and made it hard to scale.*

Will: *How's your work–life balance now?*
Ta'Nisha: *Way better. In the beginning, I missed a lot of family time. Now I set boundaries and prioritize my kids. It's okay to say no.*

Will: *What about managing income?*
Ta'Nisha: *It fluctuates. Some months are great; others are tight. I've had to learn how to manage money and not rely too much on others.*

Will: *What keeps you going?*
Ta'Nisha: *Decorating. It's my happy place. Even if it's 3 a.m., I'm at the bakery because I love it.*

Will: *This has been great. Thank you, Ta'Nisha.*

Ta'Nisha's entrepreneurial journey has transformed her into the very definition of a **Storm Chaser**—she didn't avoid the turbulence. She walked straight into it, learned from it, and built something stronger because of it. What began as a healing hobby evolved into a full-fledged business after a layoff forced her to leap. Like any resilient leader, she didn't just survive adversity—she let each storm season her grit and sharpen her instincts.

From losing her domain names to experiencing a break-in and betrayal from someone she trusted, Ta'Nisha weathered more than her fair share of storms. But with each challenge came a deeper layer of strength. She transformed a cooking show misstep into a powerful rebrand, created financial stability through discipline and learning, and reclaimed her time to be more present with her family.

What sets Ta'Nisha apart is her ability to turn pressure into power—and that's a skill every leader needs. Her story reminds us that leadership isn't about perfection or predictability. It's about showing up when the clouds roll in, learning from what hits, and building back better each time. Whether you're launching a startup, leading a team, or navigating uncertainty, the same truths apply: Trust wisely, pivot quickly, protect your peace, and never lose sight of what brings you joy.

Ta'Nisha's story left me with a few standout takeaways for anyone leading through storms.

Skills Alone Aren't Enough— Business Acumen Is Key

- Being good at a craft doesn't automatically make someone a great business owner.
- Encourage employees to develop skills beyond their technical strengths.

Build a Strong Support Network

- Having a trusted community, mentors, and peers makes a difference.
- Foster an environment where employees support each other and have access to guidance.

Stay Visible—Consistency Attracts Opportunities

- Regular engagement on social media or within professional networks opens doors.
- Support employees in building their professional presence.

Own Your Mistakes and Turn Them into Strengths

- A failure doesn't define you—how you respond does.
- Create a culture where mistakes become learning opportunities.

Prioritize Work–Life Balance

- Early sacrifices are common, but long-term success requires balance.
- Support policies that allow employees to prioritize well-being and family time.

Ta'Nisha's story offers valuable insight—but the real transformation begins when you apply these lessons to your own storm. Now it's your turn to step into the storm and reflect.

Storm-Tracking Assignment

- What early mistakes have shaped how you lead today?
- Are you visible in your networks? Where are you sharing your thought leadership?
- Who's in your support circle—and who needs to be?
- What boundaries do you need to set or reset to protect your well-being and purpose?

"IF YOUR BUSINESS ISN'T MAKING MONEY, IT'S NOT A BUSINESS; IT'S A HOBBY. MAKE SURE YOU HAVE A PRODUCT OR SERVICE THAT PEOPLE WILL PAY FOR BEFORE INVESTING TOO MUCH."

– CIANDRESS JACKSON

Ciandress Jackson, Be Great Foundation

Ciandress Jackson serves as the executive director of the Be Great Foundation, a nonprofit she founded to help historically disadvantaged youth acquire employable skills and access opportunities in STEM. Her journey is grounded in a deep sense of purpose and a lifetime of cultivating both technical expertise and community-focused leadership.

In addition to her nonprofit work, Ciandress is an accomplished IT consultant, curriculum developer, and trainer. She's developed and delivered training to over a thousand users and consistently receives high marks for her dynamic teaching and engaging content.

She's also the brilliant CTO I referenced earlier in the book.

Below is our conversation, edited for clarity and flow.

Will: *As I've shared, this book isn't a step-by-step guide—it's about the messy emotions and hard-earned lessons of entrepreneurship. Despite the struggle, there's always hope on the other side. Ciandress, what led you to start the Be Great Foundation?*
Ciandress: *Great question. I've wanted to be an entrepreneur since high school. I've had some successful ventures and some not so much. I started the Be Great Foundation to use my IT skills to make a difference. I saw a gap in STEM fields where kids—especially Black kids—weren't seeing people like them represented. I wanted to change that.*

Will: *So it started with purpose. What sparked your early interest in entrepreneurship?*

Ciandress: *In college at UVA, I felt like the traditional career paths weren't for me. So, I started a club called Young Black Entrepreneurs. We were interested in things like fashion, music, and promotion—none of which were supported at the time. That space allowed us to dream big. Many of those students are entrepreneurs now.*

Will: *What separates an entrepreneurial mindset from a traditional nine-to-five employee mindset?*

Ciandress: *Creativity. Entrepreneurs don't want to follow a formula. They want to solve problems in new ways. We thrive on freedom and innovation.*

Will: *Can you share a failure and how it impacted you?*

Ciandress: *My Club TV in 2007 was a big one. The idea was to stream nightlife experiences online—basically what influencers do now. But the market wasn't ready, and club owners didn't want the liability. I was devastated. I'd put a lot of money into it.*

Will: *It sounds like you were ahead of your time.*

Ciandress: *Totally. That was part of the frustration. But it pushed me to pivot. I started working on a children's book and animation project soon after. It helped me move forward.*

Will: *So, resilience is essential. What's a key lesson you'd offer to new entrepreneurs or entrepreneurial leaders?*

Ciandress: *Make money from the start. Passion is great, but without revenue, it's a hobby. I've learned to make sure any new idea can sustain itself financially before going all in.*

Will: *What keeps you going when things get hard?*

Ciandress: *The students at Be Great. Seeing their excitement and growth gives me purpose.*

Will: *How do you approach work–life balance?*
Ciandress: *It's a constant effort—self-care, fitness, vacations, and spending time with people inside and outside the entrepreneurial world. You have to be intentional.*

Will: *You also work in the gig economy. How do you juggle it all?*
Ciandress: *Consulting allows me to use my skills, fund my projects, and stay flexible. It's the balance I need to support my foundation, family, and myself.*

Will: *Thanks, Ciandress. This was incredibly insightful.*
Ciandress: *Thank you! I can't wait to read the book and see how others are navigating their storms.*

Ciandress's story is a portrait of what it means to be a **Storm Chaser**: someone who faces uncertainty head-on with purpose, creativity, and resolve. From founding a nonprofit to working in the gig economy, her path is defined by choice, not chance. She didn't stumble into entrepreneurship—she built it brick by brick, storm by storm.

Her journey speaks to more than just business owners. Every leader—whether in corporate, nonprofit, or creative spaces—can learn from her approach to resilience, innovation, and community-building. When one idea failed, she didn't fold—she pivoted. When she realized passion wasn't enough, she got serious about sustainability. And through it all, she stayed grounded in her mission to empower young people.

Whether you're managing a team, launching a new initiative, or navigating uncertainty, Ciandress reminds us that true leadership isn't just about vision—it's about flexibility, emotional endurance, and doing the hard work of impact.

Ciandress's story left me with a few standout takeaways for anyone leading through storms.

Purpose-Driven Leadership Creates Lasting Impact

- Leaders who align their work with a greater mission inspire teams and drive real change.
- Help employees connect their tasks to something bigger than the bottom line.

Encourage Creativity and Innovation

- Give employees permission to break the mold.
- Foster a culture that rewards experimentation and celebrates curiosity.

Perseverance Is Powerful

- Leadership is a long game.
- Normalize setbacks, celebrate resilience, and keep the mission in sight.

Ciandress's story offers valuable insight—but the real transformation begins when you apply these lessons to your own storm. Now it's your turn to step into the storm and reflect.

Storm-Tracking Assignment

- Where in your work do you need to pivot or adapt?
- Are you building a mission-driven culture—or just managing tasks?
- Do you give your employees permission to think both inside and outside the box?
- Who in your circle could benefit from mentorship, support, or representation?

"BEING AN ENTREPRENEUR MEANS OPERATING IN SPACES WHERE OTHERS MAY NOT OFTEN GO."

– ALLAN YOUNGER

Storm Chaser:
Allan Younger, GRACE Consulting

Allan works for a private foundation committed to supporting entrepreneurial ambition and economic empowerment. He oversees the foundation's programs, which provide education, training, and mentoring for individuals seeking to start and grow companies.

Allan also provides startup consulting to small business owners. He is a great connector. Allan took me around and personally introduced me to his network of business owners when I first moved to Winston Salem.

Below is our conversation, edited for clarity and flow.

Allan: *Being an entrepreneur means we're often in situations where others may not frequently go. I recently saw a meme that said, "Being in your own lane means there's not much traffic," and I think that's a good metaphor. Entrepreneurs focus on solving problems in ways others haven't considered or haven't addressed efficiently.*

Will: *Yeah, definitely.*
Allan: *And those methods may not be popular, but the goal is for people to eventually say, "I need what you're offering." I've worked with entrepreneur support organizations for years because it's hard to succeed alone. If I can share something from my journey that helps someone else, I want to do that.*

Will: *Let me ask—why do you think people go into business? You've worked with so many entrepreneurs. What patterns have you seen?*

Allan: *A few things. Some people are exposed to entrepreneurship early on—it runs in the family or community. Others see a problem that's not being addressed, often affecting underserved groups. And some people just aren't wired for traditional employment. Then you have the accidental entrepreneurs—people who lose a job or can't find the right fit and end up starting a business. Their level of commitment usually determines their success.*

Will: *That's interesting. I was an accidental entrepreneur myself after I was released from Virginia Tech. I couldn't land another job, but I always knew I'd end up working for myself. It just happened sooner than I expected.*

Allan: *Right. Eventually, people get used to managing their own time and direction. Even though you might have multiple clients or "bosses," it's different than working under one employer.*

Will: *True. Having multiple clients doesn't mean fewer demands. You're still juggling a lot.*

Allan: *Exactly. One myth is that entrepreneurs don't have a boss. In reality, they have many. And if someone treats entrepreneurship as a placeholder while they look for a job, it usually doesn't work. It takes full commitment.*

Will: *You also have to be tuned into what people need, not just what you want to offer.*

Allan: *Exactly. It's about listening. Entrepreneurs who succeed solve problems others recognize—not just problems they imagine.*

Will: *What traits do you think define successful entrepreneurs?*
Allan: *Being other-centered is huge—putting the customer's needs first. Also, humility. You need to be willing to ask for help. Risk-taking is key, too—you've got to be willing to venture into the unknown. And you must be a good communicator who can clearly convey your value.*

Will: *What kind of infrastructure helps entrepreneurs succeed?*
Allan: *A strong team. That can be a cofounder, advisors, or a supportive network. You need advocates who understand your vision and technical experts in areas where you're not strong. Nobody succeeds alone.*

Will: *So, emerging entrepreneurs need to tap into resources— grants, mentorship, technical assistance.*
Allan: *Absolutely. Every business needs fans, champions, and support.*

Will: *What advice would you give to someone working a traditional job who wants to apply entrepreneurial thinking?*
Allan: *Persistence, community, and action. Keep going even when it's hard. Build a support network. Take action—don't wait for perfect conditions. Also, be willing to take calculated risks. Growth comes from discomfort.*

Will: *You mentioned a book earlier?*
Allan: Who Owns the Ice House? *It outlines principles that help anyone succeed—entrepreneur or not. It emphasizes persistence, community, and initiative.*

Will: *I'll definitely check that out. Thanks for sharing all this, Allan.*
Allan: *My pleasure. Glad to be part of the journey.*

Allan's conversation was rich with insight and full of reminders about what it takes to lead through uncertainty. He described entrepreneurship not as a popular path but as a purposeful one—where you often find yourself in lanes no one else is traveling. That's what makes it both difficult and rewarding.

His reflections on solving real problems, building support systems, and fully committing to your path apply well beyond startups. Whether you're running a business, leading a department, or launching a project inside a corporation, Allan's lessons are universal.

Storm Chasers like Allan are marked by persistence and purpose. They step into the storm, not because it's easy but because they're driven by the belief that their work matters. And they don't do it alone—they bring others with them, build coalitions, and share what they've learned along the way.

Allan's story left me with a few standout takeaways for anyone leading through storms.

Innovation Requires Focus and a Unique Perspective

- Successful leaders solve problems in ways others might not have considered.
- Encourage employees to think creatively and take ownership of challenges within their roles.

Support and Mentorship Are Essential
- Entrepreneurs rarely succeed alone; they rely on a network of mentors and supporters.
- Foster a workplace culture where knowledge sharing, coaching, and collaboration thrive.

Identify and Solve Real Problems
- A great product or idea isn't enough—it must address a real, recognized need.
- Teach teams to actively listen to customers and stakeholders to develop relevant solutions.

Entrepreneurial Thinking Is Valuable Everywhere
- Even in traditional jobs, applying entrepreneurial principles like problem-solving, initiative, and adaptability can lead to growth.
- Encourage employees to think like entrepreneurs by fostering a culture of innovation, ownership, and continuous learning.

Allan's story offers valuable insight—but the real transformation begins when you apply these lessons to your own storm. Now it's your turn to step into the storm and reflect.

Storm-Tracking Assignment

- Are you solving real problems that others recognize—or just pushing solutions you think they need?
- Who are the advocates and mentors in your network that help you grow?
- In what ways are you building a culture of risk-taking, persistence, and action on your team?
- How can you apply entrepreneurial thinking to lead more effectively—even within a traditional role?

"I'M DRIVEN BY THE CHALLENGE. I LOVE SETTING A VISION, WORKING TOWARD IT, AND SEEING HOW FAR I CAN GO. SO, YOU ASK ME WHY, AND I SAY WHY NOT!"

– JOHN L. MERRIWEATHER

Storm Chaser:
John L. Merriweather, President and CEO, GO Destination Services

John L. Merriweather is the president and CEO of GO Destination Services, an award-winning company that provides personalized home-finding, school search, area tours, orientations, and destination services across the U.S. and hundreds of international locations.

Before founding the company in 1998, John worked in corporate training and quality management for a distribution company in Carmel, Indiana. He launched his career in the U.S. Army in 1990, where he served proudly for three years, including a tour in Operation Desert Storm.

John is a graduate of Indiana University and completed master's coursework at the University of Indianapolis, as well as executive education programs at University of Texas El Paso and the Tuck School of Business at Dartmouth.

Remember the Show Boyz? John is my childhood best friend—we started the Show Boyz together.

Below is our conversation, edited for clarity and flow.

Will: *Man, cool, cool, cool. All right, J, here's the thing. You're a business owner now, but you didn't start that way. Walk me through your journey—from Global Perspectives to GO Destination Services.*

John: *Well, thank you for the question, Dr. Lewis. I wasn't quite ready to talk about phases—like phases of the moon!*

(We both laugh. Childhood friends—you can feel it.)

Will: *See? This is why I wanted to record this—our banter is part of the story.*

John: *Okay, phases. The first one is just doing something. You start off doing it badly, then you get good, then you aim to be great. Our company has followed that path. Over the past twenty-five years, we've gone from a training and development firm to a corporate relocation company. That pivot came from recognizing opportunities, being poised to act, and executing decisively. A lot of folks talk about opportunity, but taking action is what matters.*

Will: *So, even in the beginning, were you doing work outside of your training scope just to survive?*

John: *It didn't feel like survival. It felt like expansion. When we did surveys before and after training, that led to other survey work—like for airports and zoos. We saw the opportunity and leaned in.*

Will: *So, you were opportunity-driven, not fear-driven.*

John: *Exactly. Thinking about what's possible gives me energy. Just trying to stay afloat isn't inspiring.*

Will: *And how did the big pivot to relocation services happen?*

John: *Funny story. We were talking to a large pharmaceutical company about training, which didn't pan out. But in our conversations, we discovered a need in HR—specifically, relocation services. We connected our expertise in surveys with their need to understand what relocating employees wanted in their new cities. We delivered, and it worked. So, we scaled that model.*

Will: *That's amazing. What about your failures—what didn't go so well?*

John: *Oh, plenty. Early on, we lacked market research, didn't understand our competitors, didn't seek legal or financial advice when we should have. And sometimes we gave up on processes too quickly if we didn't see immediate results. But like Henry Ford said, "The only real mistake is the one from which we learn nothing."*

Will: *So, how do you bounce back after a costly mistake?*

John: *First, make sure it doesn't happen again. That might mean updating systems, changing personnel, whatever it takes. Then, double down on marketing and internal operations. Keep moving forward.*

Will: *What role has imagination played in your growth?*

John: *A huge role. Imagination and visualization help me see where we could go next. It's not just about how we deliver today but where we could be tomorrow.*

Will: *Love it. So, what was your original "why," and is it still the same?*

John: *The why hasn't changed. Yes, there's the financial piece— bills, responsibilities—but more than that, I love the challenge. I'm driven by growth, the chance to serve iconic brands, and the question "Why not?"*

Will: *Why not? That's a perfect note to end on. Thanks, J.*

John's entrepreneurial journey is a testament to seizing opportunities, adapting through change, and constantly striving for excellence. From a childhood hustle to a global business, his story exemplifies the mindset of a true **Storm Chaser**—one who doesn't wait for conditions to be perfect but leans into uncertainty with focus and grit.

What began as a training and development firm evolved into a relocation powerhouse—not because of desperation but because John operated from vision and optimism. His ability to recognize an opportunity and pair it with swift action is a core leadership trait that applies far beyond entrepreneurship.

He's candid about his missteps—from skipping market research to prematurely abandoning strategies—but instead of letting those moments define him, he learns and adjusts. His leadership is fueled by imagination, commitment, and a belief that progress is possible even through setbacks.

Whether you're running a business or leading a team, John's lessons are clear: Stay curious, act boldly, and ask yourself not "Why?" but "Why not?"

John's story left me with a few standout takeaways for anyone leading through storms.

Growth Comes in Phases— Embrace the Process

- Every organization evolves: from doing something, to doing it badly, to doing it well, to aiming for greatness.
- Help teams see mistakes as part of the growth curve.

Opportunity and Action Must Go Hand in Hand

- Recognizing an opportunity isn't enough. Acting on it is what drives success.
- Encourage teams to act decisively, even in imperfect conditions.

Operate from Optimism, Not Fear

- Leading from a place of hope energizes teams and fosters innovation.
- Shift the mindset from "avoiding failure" to "building the future."

Imagination Fuels Innovation

- Visualizing success and crafting what *could* be is as important as meeting today's goals.
- Cultivate imagination as a leadership muscle—not just a creative trait.

John's story offers valuable insight—but the real transformation begins when you apply these lessons to your own storm. Now it's your turn to step into the storm and reflect.

Storm-Tracking Assignment

- Where in your leadership journey have you acted out of fear instead of opportunity?
- What recent opportunity did you recognize but fail to act on? Why?
- Are there ideas or strategies you abandoned too soon?
- What bold move would you make if you simply asked, "Why not?"

"FEAR KEPT ME IN PLACE FOR A LONG TIME—FEAR OF FAILURE, FINANCIAL INSECURITY, AND THE UNKNOWN. BUT EVENTUALLY, MY FRUSTRATION WITH BEING IN AN ENVIRONMENT THAT DIDN'T ALIGN WITH MY VALUES BECAME STRONGER THAN MY FEAR. THAT FRUSTRATION PUSHED ME TO TAKE THE LEAP INTO ENTREPRENEURSHIP. AND ONCE I DID, I FOUND FREEDOM—THE FREEDOM TO BUILD SOMETHING THAT REFLECTED MY VISION, MY VALUES, AND THE KIND OF WORK–LIFE BALANCE I WANTED."

– KEITH VEST

Keith Vest, The Variable

Keith Vest is chairman of The Variable, partner at 100watt, and founder of Sunshine Beverages. After running a design firm for twelve years, Keith cofounded The Variable in 2011, building on his background in design and business strategy.

Over his career, he has helped major brands grow and evolve—including Krispy Kreme, Wells Fargo, Hanesbrands, and Planters Lifesavers—and cofounded Sunshine Beverages in 2013 and 100watt in 2017.

Below is our conversation, edited for clarity and flow.

Will: *Let's start with your company. What is it, and why did you start it?*

Keith: *My background is in design. I graduated from design school with a portfolio in one hand and a business book in the other—*The Business of Graphic Design. *I spent the first decade of my career working for others, learning business operations, and imagining how I'd do things differently. Eventually, I became a junior partner in a firm, gaining real insight into running a business.*

But as my wife and I began thinking about starting a family, my values and the company culture didn't align. I was afraid—of failure, financial uncertainty, and not being able to support my family. But my frustration eventually outweighed my fear. That's when I decided to start my own venture.

I launched Pave Creative Group, a boutique firm focused on supporting marketing and sales functions. Later, I met Joe Parrish—he came from a creative director background, and I brought operational expertise. Together, we cofounded The Variable in 2011 to blend creativity with strategic business planning.

Will: *You mentioned fear, frustration, and then freedom. How did that play out?*
Keith: *Fear kept me stuck. But the misalignment in values and lifestyle made me more frustrated than afraid. Once I took the leap, I found the freedom to build something reflective of my values. Working for others gave me tools, but it was the frustration that pushed me.*

Will: *What did those first years teach you about leadership?*
Keith: *Working for others taught me that creativity alone isn't enough. You need to know how to run a business. I also learned to build a team that complements my strengths. Letting go and trusting others with key aspects of the business was critical to our growth.*

Will: *What's one of the biggest storms you've faced as a leader?*
Keith: *Around 2011–2012, we had shifted to working with larger brands. We brought in someone to lead our innovation practice, but I later found out he was committing fraud—faking clients, forging contracts. It was devastating.*

We had to decide whether to close or fight to stay open. We had four months of runway left. We were transparent with our team, and everyone chose to stay. In July 2013, we landed a major client, and things turned around. That crisis created a deeper bond within our team.

Will: What leadership lessons did you walk away with?
Keith: *Transparency is key. So is building a culture with operational integrity—putting checks and balances in place. And above all, surround yourself with good, trustworthy people.*

Will: You eventually sold part of the company. Why?
Keith: *We wanted to create something lasting. We chose private equity to grow without losing our brand identity. Around that time, I was diagnosed with stage 4 kidney cancer, which forced me to think about sustainability and succession.*

Will: Are you in remission now?
Keith: *Yes. If all continues well, I'll be five years cancer-free in September 2024. I'm incredibly grateful.*

Will: Your journey is powerful. Thank you for sharing it.

Keith's journey is a masterclass in facing fear with a cancer diagnosis, navigating betrayal, building with purpose, and stepping forward with vision. As a **Storm Chaser**, he didn't just endure high winds—he turned them into tailwinds.

From a creative professional to a seasoned CEO, Keith has built businesses that reflect his values, learned to lead through crisis, and prioritized long-term sustainability over short-term wins. His experience in cofounding The Variable, navigating internal fraud, and facing a life-altering health diagnosis has shaped a leadership approach grounded in trust, resilience, and purpose.

But Keith's lessons aren't just for entrepreneurs. Leaders across all industries can relate to his challenges: aligning vision with values, leading through crisis, and balancing ambition with well-being. His storm-chasing mindset—of leaning into risk, learning through adversity, and asking,

"Why not?"—is a model for leadership in uncertain times.

Keith's story left me with a few standout takeaways for anyone leading through storms.

Experience Is a Foundation—Build on It
- Working for others provides critical learning before launching something new.
- Encourage employees to develop business acumen, not just technical skills.

Fear and Frustration Can Be Catalysts for Growth
- Frustration with misalignment can spark bold decisions.
- Help teams recognize when it's time to change, pivot, or act on new opportunities.

Values Should Guide Business Decisions
- When leaders align work with values, the organization thrives.
- Promote clarity around mission, values, and personal alignment.

Transparency Builds Trust, Especially in Crisis
- Honest communication builds team cohesion.
- Model vulnerability and clear action plans during tough times.

Prioritize Well-Being and Succession

- Health matters—and so does planning for what comes next.
- Make room for rest, recovery, and leadership transition.

Keith's story offers valuable insight—but the real transformation begins when you apply these lessons to your own storm. Now it's your turn to step into the storm and reflect.

Storm-Tracking Assignment

- What values do you want your work—and your workplace—to reflect?
- When has fear kept you from making a change you knew you needed?
- What systems or people do you need in place to protect your business (or team) during a storm?
- Are you creating space for vision, imagination, and long-term sustainability—or just reacting to the present?

"FEAR IS A SIGNIFICANT PART OF
THE ENTREPRENEURIAL JOURNEY.
IF YOU'RE NOT AFRAID, YOU MIGHT
NOT HAVE THE HEART FOR IT."

– MAGALIE YACINTHE

Magalie Yacinthe, HUSTLE Winston-Salem

Magalie—an alumnus of Florida Agricultural and Mechanical University—was born in Nassau, Bahamas, and raised in Miami, Florida, and is one of five daughters to Haitian parents. As the senior director of programs at Forward Cities, she leads the execution and delivery of equitable entrepreneurial ecosystem-building solutions and learning engagements. She is also the founder and executive director of HUSTLE Winston-Salem, a nonprofit organization dedicated to inclusive entrepreneurship, and the creator of YES Strategies & Solutions, a consulting firm helping nonprofits and corporations implement successful programming and project management.

Below is our conversation, edited for clarity and flow.

Will: *Let's dive into our discussion. I wanted to start by asking you about fear in entrepreneurship. Fear can either push us to take action or paralyze us into inaction. How do you think fear plays a role in entrepreneurship?*
Magalie: *Fear is a significant part of the entrepreneurial journey. If you're not afraid, you might not have the heart for it. Fear is real, and it's about how you manage it. You can let it stop you, or you can push through it. Most successful entrepreneurs push through despite the fear. Whether it's the fear of uncertainty, financial risk, isolation, or the fear of failure—these are all real and present in entrepreneurship.*

Acknowledging the fear is crucial because it helps you move forward despite it. The key is not to let fear be the thing that stops you.

Will: *You've captured that so well—acknowledging fear and learning to manage it. I can see how those fears, especially around financial risk and failure, can weigh heavily on entrepreneurs, particularly those responsible for a family. I'd love your perspective on how women and men might experience and handle that fear differently.*

Magalie: *Absolutely. Women, especially those with children, often push through that fear out of necessity. But for men, particularly men of color, the fear of financial risk and failure can be suffocating. It's a lot to navigate, and it requires resilience and a willingness to face those fears head-on.*

Will: *Exactly. Sometimes you just have to "do it scared," as they say. But what happens when the thing you feared actually comes to pass? How do you bounce back from that and keep moving forward in your entrepreneurial journey?*

Magalie: *That's where resilience comes in. Entrepreneurship is like a roller coaster—it's full of ups and downs. Setbacks are inevitable, but each failure teaches you something valuable. It's important not to focus solely on the setback but rather on what you can learn from it. And that's what helps you keep going. The frustration and fear are part of the journey, but they're outweighed by the freedom that entrepreneurship ultimately brings.*

Will: *I love how you frame that. It's a roller coaster, but the freedom on the other side is worth it. Let's talk about your role as an entrepreneur. You're not only running your own business, but you're also deeply involved in supporting other entrepreneurs. Can you share more about what you do?*

Magalie: *Sure! As the executive director of HUSTLE Winston-Salem, I work directly with entrepreneurs, especially those from marginalized communities. We provide technical assistance, coaching, and resources to help them succeed. I also work with Forward Cities, where we focus on supporting the broader entrepreneurial ecosystem. This dual perspective allows me to help both individual entrepreneurs and the organizations that support them, ensuring that inclusivity and equity are at the forefront of entrepreneurship.*

Will: *That's fantastic—you're working at both the micro and mezzo levels, helping individual entrepreneurs and shaping the policies and ecosystems that support them. How do you help entrepreneurs get into the mindset of building the necessary systems and operations alongside their passion projects?*
Magalie: *It's about keeping it real with them. Many entrepreneurs get caught up in the dream and don't realize the importance of the day-to-day operations. I challenge them to think about the systems they need to put in place to sustain their business in the long run. It's not just about the fancy stuff—it's about the basics like understanding your balance sheet and profit and loss statements. I emphasize the importance of having these systems in place early on so that they're prepared to scale and succeed in the future.*

Will: *That's crucial—developing those systems is essential for long-term success. How do you think the lessons learned in entrepreneurship can be applied in a traditional business setting?*
Magalie: *The entrepreneurial mindset is not just for entrepreneurs; it's a successful mindset that can be applied in any setting. Whether you're managing a business or working in a nine-to-five role, the principles of entrepreneurship— such as assessing situations, identifying opportunities, and*

pivoting when necessary—are valuable. It's about thinking like an entrepreneur even within an existing business structure. That mindset is transferable and can help anyone succeed, regardless of their role.

Will: *I love that perspective—thinking like an entrepreneur, even if you're not one. Thank you so much for sharing your insights today, Magalie. I've learned so much from this conversation, and I'm looking forward to diving into the transcript and reflecting on everything we've discussed.*

Magalie: *You're welcome! I'm glad I could contribute, and if you have any follow-up questions, don't hesitate to reach out. I'm excited about your book and can't wait to see how it all comes together.*

Will: *Thank you, Magalie. I'll definitely keep you posted, and I'll reach out if I need any additional insights.*

Magalie's reflections illuminate what it means to be a **Storm Chaser**: someone who doesn't run from fear but acknowledges it, navigates it, and ultimately transforms it into action. Her story offers a powerful reminder that fear isn't a sign of weakness in leadership—it's often a sign you're headed toward growth.

Whether building an organization from scratch or navigating change within a corporate role, Magalie's experience proves that the core tenets of entrepreneurship—resilience, adaptability, systems thinking, and courage—are essential for any leader. She helps us see that success isn't about the absence of fear; it's about refusing to let fear be the reason you stop.

Through her leadership at HUSTLE Winston-Salem and Forward Cities, she supports inclusive innovation while equipping others with the tools to build sustainable businesses.

Her grounded advice—about managing the emotional realities of entrepreneurship, creating strong foundations, and applying the entrepreneurial mindset in any context—is applicable far beyond startup culture.

Magalie's story left me with a few standout takeaways for anyone leading through storms

Fear Is Inevitable—Managing It Is Key

- Fear exists in every career path, not just entrepreneurship.
- Encourage employees to face challenges head-on and develop strategies to work through uncertainty.

Resilience Drives Long-Term Success

- Setbacks are inevitable, but learning from them is what sets successful individuals apart.
- Foster a team culture where mistakes are seen as learning opportunities rather than failures.

Balance Passion with Practicality

- Passion drives innovation, but structure sustains it.
- Help teams focus on operational foundations like budgeting, processes, and strategic planning.

Success Requires Action, Not Just Ideas

- Vision matters, but execution delivers results.
- Encourage people to test ideas and iterate with feedback.

Magalie's story offers valuable insight—but the real transformation begins when you apply these lessons to your own storm. Now it's your turn to step into the storm and reflect.

Storm-Tracking Assignment

- When was the last time fear kept you or your team from taking action—and what would you do differently now?
- What systems and structures are in place to support your team's vision?
- How do you or your team bounce back from failure—and what does resilience look like for you?
- What steps are you taking to cultivate an entrepreneurial mindset in your team?

"WHEN I HAD KIDS, I MADE UP MY MIND THAT I DIDN'T WANT TO BE A STAY-AT-HOME MOM—I WANTED TO BE AN AVAILABLE MOM. I DIDN'T WANT TO BE CONFINED TO HOMEMAKING; I WANTED TO BE THERE FOR MY KIDS. STRUCTURING MY DAY AND BEING IN CONTROL MEANT I COULD ALSO CONTROL MY INCOME."

– LATASHA BARR-LEWIS

Latasha Barr-Lewis, Cam's Coffee Co.

Latasha Barr-Lewis is a dynamic educator, advocate, and entrepreneur. As cofounder of Cam's Coffee Co., she has leveraged her lived experiences—including raising two children with disabilities—to build a socially impactful brand that creates employment opportunities for individuals of all abilities through Full Scope, Inc. Her leadership is fueled by creativity, courage, and an unwavering commitment to family and community.

Oh, I almost forgot: Latasha is my wife (I really didn't forget, but she is going to get me for this one!).

Below is our conversation, edited for clarity and flow.

Will: *When you think about your journey into entrepreneurship, how have mindset, innovation, and creativity influenced you? How important are those elements to your entrepreneurial path?*
Latasha: *I think I show up in this space a little differently because I'm neurodivergent—I have ADHD—and I'm naturally creative. The way I approach entrepreneurship is a reflection of who I am: spontaneous, hyperactive, and creative.*

Will: *Yeah.*
Latasha: *And that shows in my business.*

Will: *So you're all over the place.*

Latasha: *True statement, and I'm not ashamed or embarrassed about it.*

Will: *Right. So, for you, innovation and creativity just come naturally, and that really fuels your entrepreneurial spirit.*

Latasha: *It does. I think it makes me better. I don't think I could work a "nine-to-five" job—there aren't many positions where you don't do the same thing every day, and I wouldn't thrive in that kind of environment.*

Will: *Got you. Before we move on to Cam's Coffee Co., I want to ask about your entrepreneurial journey. You've done a lot over the past twenty years. What sparked that entrepreneurial spirit inside you?*

Latasha: *My parents are the traditional American story— they both worked for Fortune 500 companies. My mom was a VP of tax at Wachovia, and my dad just retired from RJ Reynolds after thirty-five years. I grew up with stability, so I was never afraid to go after what I wanted. I always knew that if everything failed, I could go back home. That safety net gave me the resilience to take risks.*

Will: *So, the fear of failure wasn't really present.*

Latasha: *Right. My mom always had side hustles— catering, doing Jheri curls out of the house. As a kid, I had a Snoopy snow cone machine and was outside hustling snow cones for a quarter the day after Christmas. I rented out my bike for fifty cents an hour. I've always had hustle in me.*

Will: *And the idea of working a job for thirty years that didn't speak to your heart?*

Latasha: *That wasn't for me. As someone who's neurodivergent, I need change. The idea of someone else controlling my time was claustrophobic. Entrepreneurship gave me the flexibility to be the kind of mom I wanted to be.*

Will: *Tell me more about that—how entrepreneurship lets you be the mom you envisioned.*

Latasha: *I didn't want to be a stay-at-home mom—I wanted to be an available mom. My boys had a ton of therapy appointments. Being in control of my schedule meant I could prioritize them. If I earned less during some seasons, that was okay—my kids were the priority.*

Will: *Let's talk about Cam's Coffee Co. What is it, and how did it begin?*

Latasha: *We started when Cam was nine. It began as a hobby but grew into something sustainable—for him and others. We wanted something that could support him into adulthood if traditional work or college wasn't an option. Now, we have our own coffee beans, teas, merchandise, and a storefront that employs people with disabilities. A second location is coming soon.*

Will: *And your online presence?*

Latasha: *That saved us during COVID. We moved online, offered free ASL classes, and had over six thousand people participate in the last four years.*

Will: *Tell me about a time when something didn't go as planned.*

Latasha: *We had no professional coffee experience—it was all trial and error. People didn't take us seriously at first. Then COVID hit, and we had to close our physical locations. We didn't get Paycheck Protection Program support, but we got a* *small local grant and shared it with our employees. That moment pushed us to think bigger and hire talent outside of our region.*

Will: *So, that forced pivot expanded your reach.*
Latasha: *Exactly. And it made us rethink our whole approach. Our goal was never just to provide a job—it was to help people develop skills for independence.*

Will: *Why start your own brand now?*
Latasha: *Because there are so many families like mine—navigating fear, uncertainty, and systems that don't work. Cam got into college, but many kids don't get the same opportunities. I want to help families create opportunities for themselves and their children. One city isn't enough.*

Will: *Tell me about the time you reopened Cam's inside the Children's Museum without the money to do it.*
Latasha: *It was no different from how we started. We rarely have everything we need upfront—never have. We just figure it out. I saw a coffee shop in a lobby and made it happen. That's how I roll.*

Will: *How do you bounce back when things get tough?*
Latasha: *I let myself feel whatever I need to feel. Then I move forward. My husband—who happens to be you—is supportive, and so are our kids. I acknowledge the hard stuff, process it, and then get to work on the next step. That's resilience.*

Will: *Talk about what it's like running a family business.*
Latasha: *It's chaotic and beautiful. We live and work together. All of our kids pitch in. Some days, it's peaches and cream; some days, it's not. But I wouldn't trade it.*

I'm building something for my kids that no one else could give them.

Will: *What's it like being married to another entrepreneur?*
Latasha: *It's a roller coaster. When we're both in a low phase, we feel it. But there's mutual understanding. Not everyone with a business is an entrepreneur. If you're not growing and creating opportunities for others, it's a hobby. We're building something real—something that sustains more than just us.*

Will: *Do you make space for fun?*
Latasha: *Yes. I am a little wild, which is opposite of your structured nature. You know I bring excitement to your life! And that works!*

Will: *It definitely does. Thank you, Latasha.*
Latasha: *Pay me.*

Will: *Whatever.*

After our conversation, one truth was clear: Latasha doesn't just survive storms—she builds through them. Her story holds powerful lessons for anyone striving to lead with resilience and impact in today's unpredictable world.

Latasha emerges as a true **Storm Chaser**—not because she avoids adversity but because she meets it head-on with creativity, conviction, and deep purpose. Rather than waiting for the storm to pass, Latasha builds within it, shaping a life and business that reflect her values, her neurodivergence, and her unwavering commitment to her children and community.

Her journey into entrepreneurship wasn't born out of a textbook or a business accelerator. It was born from love, necessity, and a refusal to settle for structures that didn't fit.

Business leaders have much to learn from Latasha's story. Her example challenges conventional leadership models by reminding us that innovation often comes from lived experience. Her resilience shows that recovery is not about perfection; it's about being honest, resetting, and moving forward with grace. And her clarity of purpose reveals that leadership is ultimately about service—creating space for others to thrive even in uncertain conditions.

Latasha teaches that storms aren't detours. They are part of the path. And the leaders who succeed are the ones who keep building anyway.

Latasha's story left me with a few standout takeaways for anyone leading through storms.

Embrace Your Team's Unique Strengths

- Leaders should lean into their natural strengths and stop trying to fit into roles or routines that dim their light.
- Neurodivergence, creativity, and nonlinear thinking can be assets in uncertain environments.

Prioritize Flexibility Over Tradition

- Design your leadership life to fit your energy, purpose, and needs.
- Flexibility fuels longevity and joy in your leadership.

Empower Others

- Leadership that uplifts others becomes a movement, not just a mission.
- Make space for others to rise with you.

Stay Adaptable

- Adaptability isn't a soft skill—it's a survival skill for modern leaders.
- Leaders must shift fast when the environment changes.

Latasha's story offers valuable insight—but the real transformation begins when you apply these lessons to your own storm. Now it's your turn to step into the storm and reflect.

Storm-Tracking Assignment

- What aspects of your identity or experience might be misunderstood—and how can you use them as leadership strengths?
- Where in your work or organization are you clinging to tradition over necessary flexibility?
- How can you redesign your team's operations to empower differently abled individuals or those with untapped potential?
- When did you last pivot under pressure? What did it teach you about your resilience, creativity, and leadership style?

SECTION
Three

PART 6

LIGHTHOUSE IN THE STORM

"RESILIENT LEADERS DON'T JUST SURVIVE THE STORM; THEY SHINE THROUGH IT—SO OTHERS KNOW WHERE TO GO."

When the storm hits—when chaos swirls, visibility drops, and uncertainty tightens its grip—leaders must become the lighthouse. Not the strongest ship, not the loudest voice, not the first to react but the unwavering presence cutting through the darkness with clarity, steadiness, and purpose.

A lighthouse doesn't panic. It shines. But that beam of light doesn't cut through the darkness by accident. It requires internal clarity, a firm foundation, and the discipline of maintenance—even when weathering the worst conditions. Leaders are no different.

This final section introduces the Resilient Leader Framework—a practical, common-sense guide developed from the lived stories in this book and grounded in research on how leaders not only survive adversity but thrive through it. Think of this as both a mirror and a map: a way to see where you are and where you need to grow.

As I was writing this book, I didn't initially realize that I was creating a framework to help leaders navigate and thrive through life's storms. But when you break it down, this book is ultimately about surviving adversity—how we handle it, our mindset around it, how we grow from it, and how we ultimately thrive because of it.

As noted in a 2002 *Harvard Business Review* article, Dean Becker, founder of the resilience training firm Adaptive Learning Strategies, stated, "More than education, more than experience, more than training, a person's level of resilience will determine who succeeds and who fails. That's true in the cancer ward, it's true in the Olympics, and it's true in the boardroom" (Becker, 2002).

Research across disciplines consistently emphasizes that resilience is not only a critical leadership trait but also a catalyst for organizational effectiveness and adaptability. Resilient leaders demonstrate core attributes, such as emotional regulation, adaptability, optimism, purpose-driven focus, empathy, decisiveness, and a growth mindset (Harland et al., 2005; Southwick et al., 2017). These traits enable leaders to stay composed in times of crisis, adjust to shifting demands, and inspire confidence in others.

Studies have found that transformational and servant leadership styles are particularly effective in fostering team resilience, psychological safety, and innovation (Dartey-Baah, 2015; Wilson & Ferch, 2005). Furthermore, resilient leadership has been linked to stronger employee well-being and improved long-term performance, as leaders model behaviors that cultivate trust, emotional support, and shared vision (Everly et al., 2013; Zhang et al., 2024). Importantly, resilience is understood as a dynamic and learnable process—shaped by mindset and behavior—rather than an innate characteristic (APA, 2014). As such, resilient leadership not only sustains individuals during disruption but actively builds the organizational capacity to thrive through uncertainty.

Through analyzing the rich leadership lessons learned from the entrepreneurs featured in this book and the literature on resilience and leadership, I discovered that resiliency is the foundation of effective leadership.

At its core, seven key themes anchor what I call the Resilient Leader Framework—a guide for leaders who want to not only survive adversity but thrive because of it.

This framework equips leaders with the essential principles and actionable strategies to guide themselves and their teams through challenges while fostering long-term success.

Unlike frameworks that focus on leadership traits or inherent characteristics, the Resilient Leader Framework is built on processes and behaviors—the deliberate actions, decisions, and habits that empower leaders to navigate adversity, drive results, and create lasting impact.

The Seven Behaviors of Resilient Leaders

MINDSET MASTERY
They retain a positive and proactive outlook

ADAPTABILITY
They adjust to new circumstances and challenges

CONTINUOUS GROWTH
They embrace change and encourage improvement

7 BEHAVIORS OF RESILIENT LEADERS

EMOTIONAL INTELLIGENCE
They stay attuned to their own and others' emotions

SERVICE ORIENTED
They lead with purpose and with the needs of others in mind

STRATEGIC CAREER GROWTH
They plan for long term-growth and development

WORK–LIFE INTEGRATION
They find harmony between their work and personal lives

The Seven Behaviors of Resilient Leaders in Practice

The seven behaviors of a resilient leader—Mindset Mastery, Adaptability, Service-Oriented Leadership, Emotional Intelligence, Continuous Learning and Innovation, Strategic Career Growth, and Work–Life Integration—are not static character traits. Rather, they are dynamic, repeatable behaviors that resilient leaders intentionally practice and embody. While each behavior holds individual power, it is their collective integration that creates the internal force and external impact necessary to lead through adversity with clarity, steadiness, and purpose.

To bring these behaviors to life, I'll draw from the very process of writing this book—because nothing tested my resilience more than creating *Perched in the Storm*. What follows is a real-time, realistic view of how these behaviors show up in practice, not just in theory but in the messy, unpredictable storms of life and leadership.

Mindset Mastery

Mindset Mastery is first in the framework for a reason. Without a "Yes, I can" mindset, the other behaviors will sputter—especially when things get hard.

My first book wasn't about resilience or leadership—well, I think it loosely touched on leadership principles. It's surreal to think that I'm now writing my second book. Just three years ago, I couldn't imagine publishing even one. I always *thought* I would write a book someday, but the writing, editing, and publishing process overwhelmed me, so much so that I settled into the idea of *wanting* to write but never took real steps to make it happen.

That changed when Fabi suggested I write about my perspective on 2020. I had to have a serious conversation with myself: *Self, are you really going to do this?* It was so much easier to talk about writing than to actually sit down and do the work. And beneath the hesitation were some deeply rooted fears:

- "I'm not a writer."
- "I don't have anything new to add."
- "I'm not a big name in my field."
- "People—especially scholars and folks in higher ed—are going to judge me harshly."

To write that first book, I had to confront and dismantle those mental blocks. Even though I often preached about having a positive mindset, I had more self-doubt than I was willing to admit. I had to do the work of shifting my own thinking. That's where Fabi really helped. Together, we tackled each fear directly:

- *"I'm not a writer."* → Yes, you are. If you can put two sentences together with purpose, you're writing.
- *"I don't have anything new to add."*
  Your perspective is new. No one else has lived your story.
- *"I'm not a big name."*
  Your name carries weight anywhere because you bring value with you.
- *"People will judge me."*
  Who's your audience? If it's not higher ed scholars, then don't write for them. Write for the people you're called to serve.

Once I addressed those fears and shifted my mindset, things began to move. Writing became possible, not because my circumstances changed but because my *mindset* did. That shift didn't just allow me to write—it reshaped how I show up as a leader.

Whether you're launching a new initiative, making a tough decision, or stepping into unfamiliar territory, Mindset Mastery is the starting point. It unlocks the courage to act even when the path isn't clear—and the discipline to keep going when it gets hard.

I didn't just write one book—I wrote two. That's the kind of outcome a resilient mindset makes possible: not just survival but unexpected expansion.

The story of writing my first book highlights how shifting my mindset made the impossible feel possible. Mindset Mastery was about breaking through fear to act. But what came next—pivoting my second book midstream—required something else entirely: the courage to adapt when the path I planned no longer made sense.

Adaptability

When I think about Adaptability, I can't help but use *this* book as the anchor. Why? Because this book isn't just *about* resilience—it's a living example of it.

Let me take you back about eighteen months. I was well into writing my second book. It was focused on DEI, and, most specifically, belonging. I'd done my homework—traced the historical arc of diversity in America, made the case for why DEI still mattered (yes, even in a climate where it felt like a four-letter word)—and was shaping a message to help managers understand its ongoing value.

But then the storm rolled in. Fast. Loud. Unrelenting. The backlash against DEI didn't just bring wind and rain—it flipped the whole house upside down. And I found myself staring at a manuscript that, while important, felt like it would be washed away in the flood of outrage and misinformation. I wasn't interested in shouting into the storm or trying to patch a roof while the wind ripped it off. I'm an entrepreneur—I write to educate, to entertain, and, let's be honest, to employ. I write books to get on the stage, not just into the struggle.

So I pivoted.

I turned toward something I had been living and thinking about for a long time: the brutal, beautiful journey of entrepreneurship. I had to reckon with my own storm—my industry shifting, my pipeline drying up, my brand being solid but not stormproof. I had to ask myself the tough questions: *Can I withstand this weather? What's next if I can't?*

Some people have brands that are built like bunkers. Global reach. Massive platforms. I admire those folks. But I knew I needed to build something different—a brand that could weather the next political front *and* the next economic storm. I didn't want to just be recession-proof—I wanted to be politics-proof. That's when I realized: resilience isn't just a trait, it's a strategy.

So this book? It's my pivot. Not just in title but in essence. It's what happens when a resilient leader adapts—not by clinging tighter to a sinking ship but by learning to sail through the squall.

When I talk about Adaptability, this is what I mean. Leaders must constantly assess the conditions, read the winds, and have the courage to adjust—strategically, boldly, and sometimes painfully. This book *is* Adaptability in motion. It's a manifestation of what happens when the storm hits but you still move forward.

While Adaptability was about adjusting my approach to the storm, Service-Oriented Leadership was about remembering who I was serving in the storm. Changing the book's direction wasn't just a strategic move—it was a deeply personal act of service to my readers.

Service-Oriented Leadership

Resilient leaders know their why. Their purpose is bigger than their ego. It's what fuels their work, grounds their decisions, and keeps them steady when the skies turn dark.

When the storms hit, resilient leaders don't collapse— they harden, like stress wood. They may shift course out of necessity, but they stay true to their purpose. They keep serving their mission, their people, their teams, and their customers, no matter how rough the winds get.

When I made the decision to change the title of this book, I had to keep my why front and center. My goal has always been to inspire leaders, to offer hope, and to equip them with the knowledge and courage to walk through their own storms. I wanted this book to add as much value as possible—and I wasn't going to let the title overshadow the mission. My why had to lead the way so that I could be of service to you, a lighthouse in the storm, no matter where you are in your journey.

Service-Oriented Leadership reminded me of my mission, but Emotional Intelligence helped me deliver on that mission—by helping me manage my emotions, understand my audience, and make thoughtful, not reactive, decisions in high-stakes moments.

Emotional Intelligence

When the wind starts howling and the pressure drops, your people are looking at you. They're looking for steady hands on the wheel, calm in the chaos, and clarity in the fog. Emotional Intelligence is the inner compass that keeps us from spinning out when everything around us feels like a Category 5 crisis.

It's what helps us read the skies—read the room, the market, the mood. It helps us interpret what our team needs or what the situation demands and then respond, not with knee-jerk reactions but with grounded, strategic decisions.

Now let me be clear—we're not robots. Leaders *feel* things. We get angry. We get scared. That's normal. But Emotional Intelligence is what stops us from hurling thunderbolts at the wrong target. Just because I'm mad doesn't mean I cuss someone out in the meeting. I might go cuss in the parking lot *after* the meeting—but I keep it together during the turbulence of the storm. That's leadership.

Even something as simple as the title of this book can be a lightning rod moment. In the introduction, I talk about how I had a title I *loved*. It was personal. It meant something to me. But Emotional Intelligence made me pause and ask: *Will this connect with the people I'm trying to reach? Or will it stir up the wrong storm before they even open the first page?*

I had to recognize that what I liked personally might not land well publicly. It might stir controversy instead of conversation. So, I pivoted. I changed course. And now? I love the new title even more. I wouldn't trade it for anything—not even on a clear day.

That decision required self-awareness. It required me to manage my emotional attachment and see beyond my own perspective. That's Emotional Intelligence. That's the quiet, powerful work of resilient leadership. Even the title of this book is proof that you can adjust your sails without abandoning your mission.

Strategic Career Growth

When it comes to Strategic Career Growth, a resilient leader must always be scanning the horizon—thinking not just about today's conditions but about how to position themselves for tomorrow's opportunities. It's not enough to simply ride out the storm; you need to learn to read the clouds, anticipate the winds, and chart a course that keeps you—and your team—ahead of what's coming.

Resilient leaders don't just survive turbulent times. They emerge from them with more wisdom, more clarity, and more influence. And to do that, you can't just lead reactively—you have to lead *transformatively*. That means offering steady guidance in the present and casting a vision for the future. Someone once told me, "A great leader spends as much time in the future as they do in the present." I'd argue, spend *more* time in the future—because if you can see what's coming before the skies darken, you'll be ready when the storm hits.

That's exactly how I approached this book. Yes, it's for the world—but it's also for *me*. It's a collection of my experiences, insights, and leadership capital, gathered and shared in a way that can travel farther than I ever could alone. It's a way to scale what I know. To turn wisdom earned in the storm into something that others can learn from—something steady they can grab onto when their own skies turn gray.

And here's the career lesson: Writing this book elevated my brand. It gave me a lighthouse. It opened doors, not just because I'm Dr. Lewis but because I'm Dr. Lewis *the author*. There's a difference between introducing yourself and having someone come up to you and say, "I read your book!" That moment shifts the power dynamic. It deepens trust. It changes the entire conversation.

Strategic Career Growth isn't just about climbing the ladder inside your organization. It's about expanding your influence across your *industry* and amplifying your *personal brand*. Resilient leaders understand that their brand should not live solely within the walls of their company. Your brand should serve your organization— and your organization should support your brand. But at the end of the day, your personal brand is what anchors your credibility, your impact, and your legacy.

So ask yourself: "How am I building a brand that can stand through the storms? Am I growing in a way that strengthens both my organization and myself?" Resilient leaders don't just weather storms—they prepare, they adapt, and they grow stronger with every gust.

The decision to rename the book showed emotional control—but the broader act of writing the book at all was a strategic move to shape my influence, elevate my platform, and prepare for the opportunities ahead.

While Strategic Career Growth is about positioning yourself for influence, Continuous Growth and Innovation is about sharpening your edge—gathering the insight and innovation that keep your leadership relevant and ready for whatever storm rolls in next.

Continuous Growth and Innovation

Here's the truth: **Resilience is the currency of growth and innovation**. You can't level up without weathering some kind of storm. And storms have a way of teaching you what calm skies never could. The question isn't whether you'll be changed by the storm. You will. The real question is, how will you be changed?

What I've learned in both life and business is this: Every storm is a classroom. And every time I make it through one, I better have a new lesson in my pocket. I've had storms shake up my strategy, rattle my confidence, and even blow a few plans clean off the map. But each time, I've emerged a little wiser, a little sharper—and a whole lot more determined.

Take this book, for example. When I wrote my first one, I had a lot of passion, plenty of purpose—but I didn't quite put the pieces in place to make it move. I *thought* it was going to be part of a movement, but let's be real: It stayed a moment. A good one, but still a moment. I learned from that. I took what didn't scale, and this time, I built it into the foundation.

This book? It's not just a message. It's momentum. It's got wheels. I'm not just hoping it moves—I'm pushing it with intention, with systems, and with strategy. This is my storm-forged wisdom, shared with anyone brave enough to chase their own breakthrough.

So, here's my challenge to you: Are you growing in your storm? Are you learning while the winds blow? Are you innovating while you're dodging lightning and holding on to your hat? Because that's what resilient, entrepreneurial leaders do. They grow *in* the storm—not just after it.

And this book? It's here to help you do just that. Somewhere in these pages, I hope you find a sentence, a story, or even just a sharp one-liner that helps you not only *survive* your storm—but *thrive* in it.

So read widely. Stay curious. Carve out thirty minutes a day to explore your industry, your world, and your craft. Read books. Listen to podcasts. Learn something new every day. Because knowledge is your weather radar—and innovation is your lightning rod.

The forecast will change. Storms will come. But with the right mindset, you won't just endure them.

You'll build something stronger on the other side.

Continuous Growth and Innovation pushed me to build a book with more structure and strategy—but Work–Life Integration reminded me to protect my peace in the process. Because if you're not whole, your leadership won't hold up when the winds rise.

Work–Life Integration

Resilient leaders—really, all leaders—need to practice what we now call Work–Life Integration. (Not balance. Let's retire that word.)

Back in the day, we used to talk about work–life balance like it was some magical scale we could perfectly calibrate. But let's be honest, life and work aren't neatly separated compartments. They bleed into each other. Storms don't just hit your job or your personal life; they sweep through everything. That's why integration, not balance, is the more accurate—and more sustainable—approach.

Here's the truth: I bring my full self to work. And when I come home? I don't get to unzip my leadership jacket and leave my responsibilities at the door. Especially as an entrepreneurial leader, my work often follows me home like a determined thundercloud. And I'm okay with that—because I've learned how to blend the personal and professional in a way that doesn't burn me out.

When I was writing this book, I had to live this principle. There were moments when I had to close the laptop, take a walk, be with my family, reflect. And there were other moments—like on our Friday night Netflix-and-charcuterie dates—where my wife and I would be sitting on the couch, wine in hand, laptops open. She's watching a show, I'm editing a chapter, but we're together. That's what Work–Life Integration can look like in real time. It's not either/or. It's both/and.

Storms will demand everything from you—your time, your energy, your heart. But if you're not intentional about weaving in self-care, restoration, reflection, and rest, the storm will hollow you out from the inside. Integration means designing your life so that the wind doesn't always blow in one direction. It means having space to breathe— even when the forecast looks rough.

So, here's the bottom line: Resilient leaders don't chase balance—they cultivate harmony. They build a rhythm where their personal and professional selves don't clash like thunder but flow like rain across a landscape that's been shaped to handle it. That's what this behavior is about: creating a life where you can show up fully, weather the storm, and still have enough left in the tank to dance in the rain every now and then.

The Resilient Leader Framework:
A Diagnostic Tool for Navigating the Storm

The Resilient Leader Framework isn't just a checklist or an inspirational concept—it's a practical diagnostic tool designed to help you evaluate your leadership behaviors in real time, especially during moments of stress, change, and uncertainty.

To support your development, I developed the **Resilient Leader Self-Assessment**—a powerful tool that enables you to:

- Identify your current resilience strengths
- Uncover hidden blind spots that may be quietly holding you back
- Understand how your resilience directly impacts your team's trust, engagement, and loyalty

Your total score on the assessment will place you into one of three Resilient Leader Archetypes—each offering tailored insights and action steps to strengthen your leadership journey.

Empowered Resilient Leader

You are in the early stages of developing your resilience as a leader. This is the foundation-building phase.

- **Focus:** Strengthen Mindset Mastery, Adaptability, and Emotional Intelligence.
- **Action Step:** Identify 1–2 areas for improvement and begin practicing small, consistent habits to build resilience over time.

Strategic Resilient Leader

You have developed a solid base of resilience but may struggle with consistency across all seven behaviors.

- **Focus:** Deepen your self-awareness, refine your leadership strategies, and embrace continuous learning.
- **Action Step:** Focus on building consistency and alignment across your behaviors to unlock your next level of impact.

Transformative Resilient Leader

You demonstrate high levels of resilience, adaptability, and leadership effectiveness. You're likely seen as a role model who can lead with calm and clarity in the midst of chaos.

- **Focus:** Fine-tune your leadership approach, mentor others, and explore new ways to expand your positive influence.
- **Action Step:** Stretch beyond comfort—use your resilience to uplift others and drive change with confidence and purpose.

Go to this URL: https://s.pointerpro.com/resilientleader and take the assessment.

Use this framework as:

- A diagnostic tool to evaluate your current leadership strengths and blind spots.
- A growth map to focus your personal and professional development.
- A daily practice to help you show up as the lighthouse in someone else's storm.

Being a resilient leader doesn't mean having it all together or possessing superpowers. It means making a choice: to show up with clarity, to shine even when the conditions are rough, and to guide others forward—not perfectly but consistently.

This framework is built around seven core behaviors that I've seen in action through my own journey and in the lives of the leaders I interviewed:

- Mindset Mastery – Choosing belief over doubt, especially when the path is uncertain.
- Adaptability – Pivoting with purpose when plans change.
- Service-Oriented Leadership – Leading with the needs of others in mind.
- Emotional Intelligence – Managing your emotions so that you can lead others through theirs.
- Strategic Career Growth – Making intentional moves, even in unpredictable seasons.
- Continuous Growth and Innovation – Staying curious, evolving, and embracing new ideas.
- Work–Life Integration – Creating a life that supports, not competes with, your leadership.

Before you close this book, take a moment to reflect—honestly and without judgment.

These questions are your final storm-tracking assignment:

- Which behaviors are your current strengths?
- Which behaviors do you struggle with under stress or avoid altogether?
- Where have you seen the most growth in the last year?
- What's one area that could change the game if you gave it serious attention?

Your storms may not be over—but now, you have a framework to navigate them with purpose.

EPILOGUE

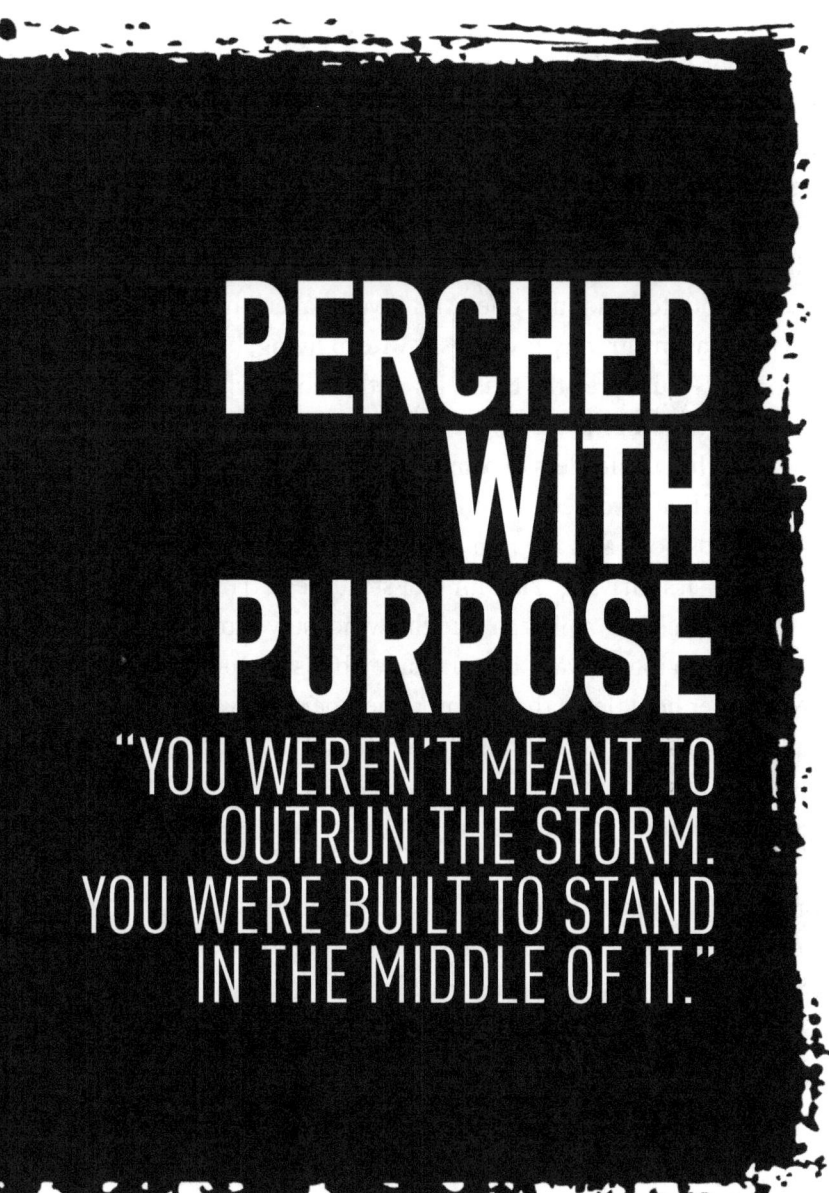

PERCHED WITH PURPOSE

"YOU WEREN'T MEANT TO OUTRUN THE STORM. YOU WERE BUILT TO STAND IN THE MIDDLE OF IT."

All right, let's get one thing straight. This book isn't just about surviving the storm. Oh no. It's about honoring resilience: the unshakable will to endure and the fierce determination to never, ever give up. It's about emerging from chaos not unscathed—because let's be honest, like the bird on the cover, you will be shaken—but stronger, more grounded, and far more prepared for whatever comes next.

Resilient One, here's the deal: Storms are part of the human experience. You're either in one, coming out of one, or about to head into one. And if you haven't hit a storm yet, as my granny used to say, "Keep living, baby— it's coming." But here's the truth: It's in the storm where we learn what we're made of. It's in those tough, stretching moments that the leaders of tomorrow are forged.

Think of that bird perched on the branch, holding steady as the winds howl and the rain beats down. It's not just surviving—it's thriving. That kind of steadiness? That's your strength. Your ability to face the wind, stay grounded, and keep moving forward is your leadership superpower.

No matter how fierce the storm, remember, you were made for this. You weren't built to run from the storm. You were built to stand in it.

So, as you move forward, don't just leave these lessons behind. Carry them with you like an umbrella and a compass. Embrace the storm because each one is shaping you into a stronger, wiser, and more resilient leader.

Stand tall. Lead with purpose. And, when the sky clears, rise—because you will.

You were perched with purpose. Now fly.

REFERENCES

Introduction

American Psychological Association. (2014). *The Road to Resilience.* https://www.apa.org/topics/resilience

Niklas, K. J. (1992). *Plant biomechanics: An engineering approach to plant form and function.* University of Chicago Press.

Schwab, K. (2016). *The Fourth Industrial Revolution.* World Economic Forum. https://www.weforum.org/about/the-fourth-industrial-revolution-by-klaus-schwab

Telewski, F. W. (1995). *Wind-induced physiological and developmental responses in trees.* In M. P. Coutts & J. Grace (Eds.), Wind and trees (pp. 237–263). Cambridge University Press.

Part 1: Eye of the Idea

Alsbrooks, B. (n.d.). *Blessed and Unstoppable* [YouTube video]. https://youtu.be/kqYPeQZfpb8

Plato. (1991). *The Republic* (A. Bloom, Trans.). Basic Books. (Original work written ca. 380 BCE).

Wachowski, L., & Wachowski, L. (Writers & Directors). (1999). *The Matrix* [Film]. Warner Bros.

Part 2: Direct Hit

Díaz del Castillo, B. (1963). *The Conquest of New Spain* (J. M. Cohen, Trans.). Penguin Classics. (Original work published 1568).

Part 3: A Perfect Storm

Junger, S. (1997). *The Perfect Storm: A True Story of Men Against the Sea.* W.W. Norton & Company.

National Weather Service. (n.d.). *The Perfect Storm,* October 1991. NOAA. https://www.weather.gov/box/oct1991storm

Part 4: Rebuilding in the Rain

The Holy Bible, New King James Version. (1982). Thomas Nelson. (Original work published 1611).

Part 6: Lighthouse

Becker, D. (2002). The Resilient Leader. *Harvard Business Review,* 80(5), 3–5.

Dartey-Baah, K. (2015). Resilient leadership: A transformational–transactional leadership mix. *Journal of Global Responsibility,* 6(1), 99–112.

Everly, G. S., Smith, K. J., & Lobo, R. (2013). Resilient leadership and the organizational culture of resilience: Construct validation. *International Journal of Emergency Mental Health,* 15(2), 123–128.

Harland, L., Harrison, W., Jones, J. R., & Reiter-Palmon, R. (2005). Leadership behaviors and subordinate resilience. *Journal of Leadership & Organizational Studies,* 11(2), 2–14.

Southwick, S. M., Martini, B., Charney, D. S., & Southwick, F. (2017). *Leadership and resilience.* In Leadership Today (pp. 199–213). Springer.

Wilson, M., & Ferch, S. R. (2005). Enhancing resilience in the workplace through the practice of servant leadership. *Organization Development Journal,* 23(4), 45–60.

Zhang, J., Xie, C., & Huang, S. S. (2024). The effect of resilient leadership on employee resilience during a crisis in tourism & hospitality firms: A self-determination perspective. *International Journal of Hospitality Management,* Volume 122, September 202, p.103886

This book was proudly published by:

SPARK
PUBLICATIONS

Expertly crafted publications for leaders building impact, celebrating milestones, or preserving their legacy.

SPARK Publications is a consulting, creative, and production firm specializing in high-end books, magazines, and catalogs for leaders and organizations ready to share their expertise and stories with purpose.

Our publishing paths meet leaders at every stage of their journey—from fully custom, high-touch projects (anniversary books, coffee-table, cookbooks, business books) to fractional self-publishing support and purpose-driven memoir development.

Memoirs That Move™
Move hearts. Move missions. Move businesses.
For purpose-driven leaders ready to turn lived experiences into memoirs, platforms, and movements that inspire others and shape what's next.

SPARK Digital Design®
Fractional self-publishing services for professionally produced books—your story, expertly guided and beautifully finished.

SPARKpublications.com

Let us know that William Lewis sent you our way!

CAMS
COFFEE CO.

Cam's Coffee Co.
Brewing Resilience, One Cup at a Time

When life gives you challenges, resilience is what carries you through. Cam's Coffee Co. was founded on that very principle.

At just nine years old, Camden Myers—a young entrepreneur with a traumatic brain injury—chose not to be defined by his limitations. Instead, he created a business that empowers others with disabilities through meaningful employment and community impact.

Today, Cam's Coffee Co. is more than a coffee shop. It's a social enterprise where every latte, every pastry, and every smile represents resilience, inclusion, and possibility. From our signature Queen Bee latte to our community training programs, we are proof that purpose and perseverance can build something extraordinary.

Because resilience isn't just surviving. It's creating. It's thriving. It's brewing hope for tomorrow—one cup at a time.

Visit us at
Camscoffeecreations.com

Follow the movement:
@CamsCoffeeCo
#CamFam | #ImWithCam

Meet William

Dr. William T. Lewis, Sr., is a nationally recognized thought leader in organizational culture, leadership, and change management. He is the award-winning author of *Sweet Potato or Pumpkin Pie: Conversations with My White Friends about Race* and *Perched in the Storm: Brutal Lessons in Resilience Every Leader Can Learn from Entrepreneurs.*

A Marine Corps veteran and "Chief Executive Gopher" of his family's social enterprise, Cam's Coffee Co., Dr. Lewis champions inclusive employment for individuals with disabilities. With a PhD in higher education administration and a master's in social work, he anchors his work in belonging, service, and resilience.

Stay Connected

wtlewis.com

wtlewis.com/podcast

william@wtlewis.com